1 CORINTHIANS

1 Corinthians

A LIFE APPLICATION® BIBLE STUDY

Part 1:
Complete text of 1 Corinthians with study notes
from the *Life Application Bible*

Part 2:
Thirteen lessons for individual or group study

Study questions written and edited by
MIKE MARCEY
DARYL J. LUCAS
DR. JAMES C. GALVIN
REV. DAVID R. VEERMAN
DR. BRUCE B. BARTON

Tyndale House Publishers, Inc.
Wheaton, Illinois

Life Application Bible Studies

Genesis TLB

Joshua TLB

Judges NIV

Ruth & Esther TLB

1 Samuel NIV

Ezra & Nehemiah NIV

Proverbs NIV

Daniel NIV

Hosea & Jonah TLB

Mark TLB

John NIV

Acts TLB

Romans NIV

1 Corinthians NIV

Galatians & Ephesians NIV

Philippians & Colossians NIV

1 & 2 Timothy & Titus NIV

Hebrews NIV

James NIV

Revelation NIV

Life Application Bible Studies: 1 Corinthians. Copyright © 1991 by Tyndale House Publishers, Inc., Wheaton. IL 60189

Life Application is a registered trademark of Tyndale House Publishers, Inc.

The text of 1 Samuel is from *The Holy Bible,* New International Version. Copyright © 1973, 1978, 1984 by International Bible Society. Used by permission of Zondervan Publishing House. All rights reserved.

Life Application Notes and Bible Helps © 1986 owned by assignment by Tyndale House Publishers, Inc., Wheaton, IL 60189. Maps © 1986 by Tyndale House Publishers, Inc. All rights reserved.

Front cover photo copyright © 1990 by A. Hubrich/H. Armstrong Roberts

ISBN 0-8423-2735-5

Printed in the United States of America

97 96 95 94 93 92 91
7   6   5   4   3   2   1

This book of 1 Corinthians is part of the *New International Version* of the Holy Bible, a completely new translation made by over a hundred scholars working directly from the best available Greek texts. It had its beginning in 1965 when, after several years of exploratory study by committees from the Christian Reformed Church and the National Association of Evangelicals, a group of scholars met at Palos Heights, Illinois, and concurred in the need for a new translation of the Bible in contemporary English. This group, though not made up of official church representatives, was transdenominational. Its conclusion was endorsed by a large number of leaders from many denominations who met in Chicago in 1966.

Responsibility for the new version was delegated by the Palos Heights group to a self-governing body of fifteen, the Committee on Bible Translation, composed for the most part of biblical scholars from colleges, universities and seminaries. In 1967 the New York Bible Society (now the International Bible Society) generously undertook the financial sponsorship of the project—a sponsorship that made it possible to enlist the help of many distinguished scholars. The fact that participants from the United States, Great Britain, Canada, Australia and New Zealand worked together gave the project its international scope. That they were from many denominations—including Anglican, Assemblies of God, Baptist, Brethren, Christian Reformed, Church of Christ, Evangelical Free, Lutheran, Mennonite, Methodist, Nazarene, Presbyterian, Wesleyan, and other churches—helped to safeguard the translation from sectarian bias.

How it was made helps to give the New International Version its distinctiveness. The translation of each book was assigned to a team of scholars. Next, one of the Intermediate Editorial Committees revised the initial translation, with constant reference to the Hebrew, Aramaic, or Greek. Their work then went to one of the General Editorial Committees, which checked it in detail and made another thorough revision. This revision in turn was carefully reviewed by the Committee on Bible Translation, which made further changes and then released the final version for publication. In this way the entire Bible underwent three revisions, during each of which the translation was examined for its faithfulness to the original languages and for its English style.

All this involved many thousands of hours of research and discussion regarding the meaning of the texts and the precise way of putting them into English. It may well be that no other translation has been made by a more thorough process of review and revision from committee to committee than this one.

From the beginning of the project, the Committee on Bible Translation held to certain goals for the New International Version: that it would be an accurate translation and one that would have clarity and literary quality and so prove suitable for public and private reading, teaching, preaching, memorizing and liturgical use. The Committee also sought to preserve some measure of continuity with the long tradition of translating the Scriptures into English.

In working toward these goals, the translators were united in their commitment to the authority and infallibility of the Bible as God's Word in written form. They believe that it contains the divine answer to the deepest needs of humanity, that it sheds unique light on our path in a dark world, and that it sets forth the way to our eternal well-being.

The first concern of the translators has been the accuracy of the translation and its fidelity to the thought of the biblical writers. They have striven for more than a word-for-word translation. Because thought patterns and syntax differ from language to language, faithful communication of the meaning of the writers of the Bible demands frequent modifications in sentence structure and constant regard for the contextual meanings of words.

The Committee on Bible Translation submitted the developing version to a number of stylistic consultants. Samples of the translation were tested for clarity and ease of reading by various kinds of people—young and old, highly educated and less well educated, ministers and laymen. Concern for clear and natural English motivated the translators and consultants. In view of the international use of English, the translators sought to avoid obvious Americanisms on the one hand and obvious Anglicisms on the other. A British edition reflects the comparatively few differences of significant idiom and of spelling.

As for the traditional pronouns "thou," "thee" and "thine" in reference to the Deity, the translators judged that to use these archaisms (along with the old verb forms such as "doest," "wouldest" and "hadst") would violate accuracy in translation. Greek does not use special pronouns for the persons of the Godhead. A present-day translation is not enhanced by forms that in the time of the King James Version were used in everyday speech, whether referring to God or man.

The Greek text used in translating the New Testament was an eclectic one. No other piece of ancient literature has such an abundance of manuscript witnesses as does the New Testament. Where existing manuscripts differ, the translators made their choice of readings according to accepted principles of New Testament textual criticism. Footnotes call attention to places where there was uncertainty about what the original text was. The best current printed texts of the Greek New Testament were used.

There is a sense in which the work of translation is never wholly finished. This applies to all great literature and uniquely so to the Bible. In 1973 the New Testament in the New International Version was published. Since then, suggestions for corrections and revisions have been received from various sources. The Committee on Bible Translation carefully considered the suggestions and adopted a number of them. These were incorporated in the first printing of the entire Bible in 1978. Additional revisions were made by the Committee on Bible Translation in 1983 and appear in printings after that date.

To achieve clarity the translators sometimes supplied words not in the original texts but required by the context. If there was uncertainty about such material, it is enclosed in brackets. Also for the sake of clarity or style, nouns, including some proper nouns, are sometimes substituted for pronouns, and vice versa. As an aid to the reader, italicized sectional headings are inserted in most of the books. They are not to be regarded as part of the NIV text, are not for oral reading, and are not intended to dictate the interpretation of the sections they head.

The footnotes in this version are of several kinds, most of which need no explanation. Those giving alternative translations begin with "Or" and generally introduce the alternative with the last word preceding it in the text, except when it is a single-word alternative; in poetry quoted in a footnote a slant mark indicates a line division. Footnotes introduced by "Or" do not have uniform significance. In some cases two possible translations were considered to have about equal validity. In other cases, though the translators were convinced that the translation in the text was correct, they judged that another interpretation was possible and of sufficient importance to be represented in a footnote. In the New Testament, footnotes that refer to uncertainty regarding the original text are introduced by "Some manuscripts" or similar expressions.

It should be noted that minerals, flora and fauna, architectural details, articles of clothing and jewelry, musical instruments and other articles cannot always be identified with precision. Also, measures of capacity in the biblical period are particularly uncertain.

Like all translations of the Bible, made as they are by imperfect man, this one undoubtedly falls short of its goals. Yet we are grateful to God for the extent to which he has enabled us to realize these goals and for the strength he has given us and our colleagues to complete our task. We offer this version of the Bible to him in whose name and for whose glory it has been made. We pray that it will lead many into a better understanding of the Holy Scriptures and a fuller knowledge of Jesus Christ the incarnate Word, of whom the Scriptures so faithfully testify.

The Committee on Bible Translation

June 1978
(Revised August 1983)

Names of the translators and editors may be secured
from the International Bible Society,
translation sponsors of the New International Version,
P.O. Box 62970, Colorado Springs, Colorado, 80962-2970 U.S.A.

The New International Version has one of the most accurate and best-organized cross-reference systems available.

The cross-references link words or phrases in the NIV text with counterpart Biblical references listed in a side column on every page. The raised letters containing these cross-references are set in a light italic typeface to distinguish them from the NIV text note letters, which use a bold typeface.

The lists of references are in Biblical order with one exception: If reference is made to a verse within the same chapter, that verse (indicated by "ver") is listed first.

In the Old Testament, some references are marked with an asterisk (*), which means that the Old Testament verse or phrase is quoted in the New Testament (see, for example, Genesis 1:3).

Following is a list of abbreviations used in the cross-references:

ABBREVIATIONS FOR THE BOOKS OF THE BIBLE

Genesis . . . . Ge	Isaiah . . . . Isa	Romans . . . . Ro
Exodus . . . . Ex	Jeremiah . . . . Jer	1 Corinthians 1Co
Leviticus . . . . .Lev	Lamentations . . . . La	2 Corinthians 2Co
Numbers . . . . Nu	Ezekiel . . . . Eze	Galatians . . . . .Gal
Deuteronomy . . . . .Dt	Daniel . . . . .Da	Ephesians . . . . Eph
Joshua . . . . Jos	Hosea . . . . Hos	Philippians . . . . Php
Judges . . . . Jdg	Joel . . . . .Joel	Colossians . . . . .Col
Ruth . . . . Ru	Amos . . . . Am	1 Thessalonians 1Th
1 Samuel 1Sa	Obadiah . . . . .Ob	2 Thessalonians 2Th
2 Samuel 2Sa	Jonah . . . . Jnh	1 Timothy 1Ti
1 Kings 1Ki	Micah . . . . .Mic	2 Timothy 2Ti
2 Kings 2Ki	Nahum . . . . .Na	Titus . . . . Tit
1 Chronicles 1Ch	Habakkuk . . . . .Hab	Philemon . . . . .Phm
2 Chronicles 2Ch	Zephaniah . . . . Zep	Hebrews . . . . Heb
Ezra . . . . Ezr	Haggai . . . . .Hag	James . . . . Jas
Nehemiah . . . . Ne	Zechariah . . . . Zec	1 Peter 1Pe
Esther . . . . Est	Malachi . . . . .Mal	2 Peter 2Pe
Job . . . . Job	Matthew . . . . .Mt	1 John 1Jn
Psalms . . . . Ps	Mark . . . . Mk	2 John 2Jn
Proverbs . . . . Pr	Luke . . . . Lk	3 John 3Jn
Ecclesiastes . . . . .Ecc	John . . . . Jn	Jude . . . . .Jude
Song of Songs . . . . SS	Acts . . . . .Ac	Revelation . . . . Rev

NOTES
In addition to providing the reader with many application notes, the *Life Application Bible* offers several explanatory notes that help the reader understand culture, history, context, difficult-to-understand passages, background, places, theological concepts, and the relationship of various passages in Scripture to other passages.

BOOK INTRODUCTION
The Book Introduction is divided into several easy-to-find parts:

Timeline. A guide that puts the Bible book into its historical setting. It lists the key events and the dates when they occurred.

Vital Statistics. A list of straight facts about the book—those pieces of information you need to know at a glance.

Overview. A summary of the book with general lessons and applications that can be learned from the book as a whole.

Blueprint. The outline of the book. It is printed in easy-to-understand language and is designed for easy memorization. To the right of each main heading is a key lesson that is taught in that particular section.

Megathemes. A section that gives the main themes of the Bible book, explains their significance, and then tells why they are still important for us today.

Map. If included, this shows the key places found in that book and retells the story of the book from a geographical perspective.

OUTLINE
The *Life Application Bible* has a new, custom-made outline that was designed specifically from an application point of view. Several unique features should be noted:

1. To avoid confusion and to aid memory work, the book outline has only three levels for headings. Main outline heads are marked with a capital letter. Subheads are marked by a number. Minor explanatory heads have no letter or number.

2. Each main outline head marked by a letter also has a brief paragraph below it summarizing the Bible text and offering a general application.

3. Parallel passages are listed where they apply.

PERSONALITY PROFILES

Another unique feature of this Bible is the profiles of key Bible people, including their strengths and weaknesses, greatest accomplishments and mistakes, and key lessons from their lives.

MAPS

The *Life Application Bible* has a thorough and comprehensive Bible atlas built right into the book. There are two kinds of maps: A book introduction map, telling the story of the book, and thumbnail maps in the notes, plotting most geographic movements.

CHARTS AND DIAGRAMS

Many charts and diagrams are included to help the reader better visualize difficult concepts or relationships. Most charts not only present the needed information but show the significance of the information as well.

CROSS-REFERENCES

A carefully organized cross-reference system in the margins of the Bible text helps the reader find related passages quickly.

HIGHLIGHTED NOTES

In each Bible study lesson you will be asked to read specific notes as part of your preparation. These notes have been highlighted by a bullet (•) so that you can find them easily.

Have you ever opened your Bible and asked the following:

- What does this passage really mean?
- How does it apply to my life?
- Why does some of the Bible seem irrelevant?
- What do these ancient cultures have to do with today?
- I love God; why can't I understand what he is saying to me through his Word?
- What's going on in the lives of these Bible people?

Many Christians do not read the Bible regularly. Why? Because in the pressures of daily living they cannot find a connection between the timeless principles of Scripture and the ever-present problems of day-by-day living.

God urges us to apply his Word (Isaiah 42:23; 1 Corinthians 10:11; 2 Thessalonians 3:4), but too often we stop at accumulating Bible knowledge. This is why the *Life Application Bible* was developed—to show how to put into practice what we have learned.

Applying God's Word is a vital part of one's relationship with God; it is the evidence that we are obeying him. The difficulty in applying the Bible is not with the Bible itself, but with the reader's inability to bridge the gap between the past and present, the conceptual and practical. When we don't or can't do this, spiritual dryness, shallowness, and indifference are the results.

The words of Scripture itself cry out to us, "Do not merely listen to the word, and so deceive yourselves. Do what it says" (James 1:22). The *Life Application Bible* helps us do just that. Developed by an interdenominational team of pastors, scholars, family counselors, and a national organization dedicated to promoting God's Word and spreading the gospel, the *Life Application Bible* took many years to complete, and all the work was reviewed by several renowned theologians under the directorship of Dr. Kenneth Kantzer.

The *Life Application Bible* does what a good resource Bible should—it helps you understand the context of a passage, gives important background and historical information, explains difficult words and phrases, and helps you see the interrelationship of Scripture. But it does much more. The *Life Application Bible* goes deeper into God's Word, helping you discover the timeless truth being communicated, see the relevance for your life, and make a personal application. While some study Bibles attempt application, over 75 percent of this Bible is application oriented. The notes answer the questions, "So what?" And "What does this passage mean to me, my family, my friends, my job, my neighborhood, my church, my country?"

Imagine reading a familiar passage of Scripture and gaining fresh insight, as if it were the first time you had ever read it. How much richer your life would be if you left each Bible reading with a new perspective and a small change for the better. A small change every day adds up to a changed life—and that is the very purpose of Scripture.

The best way to define application is to first determine what it is *not*. Application is *not* just accumulating knowledge. This helps us discover and understand facts and concepts, but it stops there. History is filled with philosophers who knew what the Bible said but failed to apply it to their lives, keeping them from believing and changing. Many think that understanding is the end goal of Bible study, but it is really only the beginning.

Application is *not* just illustration. Illustration only tells us how someone else handled a similar situation. While we may empathize with that person, we still have little direction for our personal situation.

Application is *not* just making a passage "relevant." Making the Bible relevant only helps us to see that the same lessons that were true in Bible times are true today; it does not show us how to apply them to the problems and pressures of our individual lives.

What, then, is application? Application begins by knowing and understanding God's Word and its timeless truths. *But you cannot stop there.* If you do, God's Word may not change your life, and it may become dull, difficult, tedious, and tiring. A good application focuses the truth of God's Word, shows the reader what to do about what is being read, and motivates the reader to respond to what God is teaching. All three are essential to application.

Application is putting into practice what we already know (see Mark 4:24 and Hebrews 5:14) and answering the question "So what?" by confronting us with the right questions and motivating us to take action (see 1 John 2:5, 6 and James 2:26). Application is deeply personal—unique for each individual. It is making a relevant truth a personal truth and involves developing a strategy and action plan to live your life in harmony with the Bible. It is the Biblical "how to" of life.

You may ask, "How can your application notes be relevant to *my* life?" Each application note has three parts: (1) an *explanation* that ties the note directly to the Scripture passage and sets up the truth that is being taught, (2) the *bridge* that explains the timeless truth and makes it relevant for today, (3) the *application* that shows you how to take the timeless truth and apply it to your personal situation. No note, by itself, can apply Scripture directly to your life. It can only teach, direct, lead, guide, inspire, recommend, and urge. It can give you the resources and direction you need to apply the Bible; but only *you* can take these resources and put them into practice.

A good note, therefore, should not only give you knowledge and understanding but point you to application. Before you buy any kind of resource study Bible, you should evaluate the notes and ask the following questions: (1) Does the note contain enough information to help me understand the point of the Scripture passage? (2) Does the note assume I know too much? (3) Does the note avoid denominational bias? (4) Do the notes touch most of life's experiences? (5) Does the note help me *apply* God's Word?

ON A BED of grass, a chameleon's skin turns green. On the earth, it becomes brown. The animal changes to match the environment. Many creatures blend into nature with God-given camouflage suits to aid their survival. It's natural to fit in and adapt to the environment. But followers of Christ are *new creations*, born from above and changed from within, with values and life-styles that confront the world and clash with accepted morals. True believers don't blend in very well.

The Christians in Corinth were struggling with their environment. Surrounded by corruption and every conceivable sin, they felt the pressure to adapt. They knew they were free in Christ, but what did this freedom mean? How should they view idols or sexuality? What should they do about marriage, women in the church, and the gifts of the Spirit? These were more than theoretical questions—the church was being undermined by immorality and spiritual immaturity. The believers' faith was being tried in the crucible of immoral Corinth, and some of them were failing the test.

Paul heard of their struggles and wrote this letter to address their problems, heal their divisions, and answer their questions. Paul confronted them with their sin and their need for corrective action and clear commitment to Christ.

After a brief introduction (1:1–9), Paul immediately turns to the question of unity (1:10—4:21). He emphasizes the clear and simple gospel message around which all believers should rally; he explains the role of church leaders; and he urges them to grow up in their faith.

Paul then deals with the immorality of certain church members and the issue of lawsuits among Christians (5:1—6:8). He tells them to exercise church discipline and to settle their internal matters themselves. Because so many of the problems in the Corinthian church involved sex, Paul denounces sexual sin in the strongest possible terms (6:9–20).

Next Paul answers some questions that the Corinthians had. Because prostitution and immorality were pervasive, marriages in Corinth were in shambles, and Christians weren't sure how to react. Paul gives pointed and practical answers (7:1–40). Concerning the question of meat sacrificed to idols, Paul suggests that we show complete commitment to Christ and sensitivity to other believers, especially weaker brothers and sisters (8:1—11:2).

Paul goes on to talk about worship, and he carefully explains the role of women, the Lord's Supper, and spiritual gifts (11:3—14:39). Sandwiched in the middle of this section is his magnificent description of the greatest gift—love (chapter 13). Then Paul concludes with a discussion of the resurrection (15:1–58), some final thoughts, greetings, and a benediction (16:1–24).

In this letter Paul confronted the Corinthians about their sins and shortcomings. And 1 Corinthians calls all Christians to be careful not to blend in with the world and accept its values and life-styles. We must live Christ-centered, blameless, loving lives that make a difference for God. As you read 1 Corinthians, examine your values in light of complete commitment to Christ.

VITAL STATISTICS

PURPOSE:
To identify problems in the Corinthian church, to offer solutions, and to teach the believers how to live for Christ in a corrupt society

AUTHOR:
Paul

TO WHOM WRITTEN:
The church in Corinth, and Christians everywhere

DATE WRITTEN:
About A.D. 55, near the end of Paul's three-year ministry in Ephesus, during his third missionary journey

SETTING:
Corinth was a major cosmopolitan city, a seaport and major trade center—the most important city in Achaia. It was also filled with idolatry and immorality. The church was largely made up of Gentiles. Paul had established this church on his second missionary journey.

KEY VERSE:
"I appeal to you, brothers, in the name of our Lord Jesus Christ, that all of you agree with one another so that there may be no divisions among you and that you may be perfectly united in mind and thought" (1:10).

KEY PEOPLE:
Paul, Timothy, members of Chloe's household

KEY PLACES:
Worship meetings in Corinth

SPECIAL FEATURES:
This is a strong, straightforward letter.

THE BLUEPRINT

A. PAUL ADDRESSES CHURCH PROBLEMS
(1:1—6:20)
1. Divisions in the church
2. Disorder in the church

Without Paul's presence, the Corinthian church had fallen into divisiveness and disorder. This resulted in many problems, which Paul addressed squarely. We must be concerned for unity and order in our local churches, but we should not mistake inactivity for order and cordiality for unity. We too must squarely address problems in our churches.

B. PAUL ANSWERS CHURCH QUESTIONS
(7:1—16:24)
1. Instruction on Christian marriage
2. Instruction on Christian freedom
3. Instruction on public worship
4. Instruction on the resurrection

The Corinthians had sent Paul a list of questions, and he answered them in a way meant to correct abuses in the church and to show how important it is that they live what they believe. Paul gives us a Christian approach to problem-solving. He analyzed the problem thoroughly to uncover the underlying issue and then highlighted the Biblical values that should guide our actions.

MEGATHEMES

THEME	EXPLANATION	IMPORTANCE
Loyalties	The Corinthians were rallying around various church leaders and teachers—Peter, Paul, and Apollos. These loyalties led to intellectual pride and created a spirit of division in the church.	Our loyalty to human leaders or human wisdom must never divide Christians into camps. We must care for our fellow believers, not fight with them. Your allegiance must be to Christ. Let him lead you.
Immorality	Paul received a report of uncorrected sexual sin in the church at Corinth. The people had grown indifferent to immorality. Others had misconceptions about marriage. We are to live morally, keeping our bodies ready to serve God at all times.	Christians must never compromise with sinful ideas and practices. We should not blend in with people around us. You must live up to God's standard of morality and not condone immoral behavior even if society accepts it.
Freedom	Paul taught freedom of choice on practices not expressly forbidden in Scripture. Some believers felt certain actions—like eating the meat of animals used in pagan rituals—were corrupt by association. Others felt free to participate in such actions without feeling that they had sinned.	We are free in Christ, yet we must not abuse our Christian freedom by being inconsiderate and insensitive to others. We must never encourage others to do wrong because of something we have done. Let love guide your behavior.
Worship	Paul addressed disorder in worship. People were taking the Lord's Supper without first confessing sin. There was misuse of spiritual gifts and confusion over women's roles in the church.	Worship must be carried out properly and in an orderly manner. Everything we do to worship God should be done in a manner worthy of his high honor. Make sure that worship is harmonious, useful, and edifying to all believers.
Resurrection	Some people denied that Christ rose from the dead. Others felt that people would not physically be resurrected. Christ's resurrection assures us that we will have new, living bodies after we die. The hope of the resurrection forms the secret of Christian confidence.	Since we will be raised again to life after we die, our lives are not in vain. We must stay faithful to God in our morality and our service. We are to live today knowing we will spend eternity with Christ.

A. PAUL ADDRESSES CHURCH PROBLEMS (1:1 — 6:20)

Through various sources, Paul had received reports of problems in the Corinthian church, including jealousy, divisiveness, sexual immorality, and failure to discipline members. Churches today must also address the problems they face. We can learn a great deal by observing how Paul handled these delicate situations.

1:1
a Ro 1:1
b 2Co 1:1

1 Paul, called to be an apostle*a* of Christ Jesus by the will of God,*b* and our brother Sosthenes,

1:2
c Ro 1:7

2To the church of God in Corinth, to those sanctified in Christ Jesus and called*c*

CORINTH AND EPHESUS
Paul wrote this letter to Corinth during his three-year visit in Ephesus on his third missionary journey. The two cities sat across from each other on the Aegean Sea—both were busy and important ports. Titus may have carried this letter from Ephesus to Corinth (2 Corinthians 12:18).

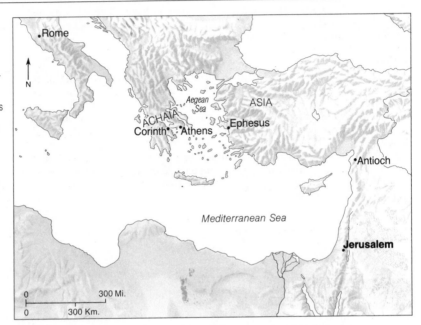

- **1:1** Paul wrote this letter to the church in Corinth while he was visiting Ephesus during his third missionary journey (Acts 19:1 — 20:1). Corinth and Ephesus faced each other across the Aegean Sea. Paul knew the Corinthian church well because he had spent 18 months in Corinth during his second missionary journey (Acts 18:1–18). While in Ephesus, he had heard about problems in Corinth (1:11). About the same time, a delegation from the Corinthian church had visited Paul to ask his advice about their conflicts (16:17). Paul's purpose for writing was to correct those problems and to answer questions church members had asked in a previous letter (7:1).

- **1:1** Paul was given a special calling from God to preach about Jesus Christ. Each Christian has a job to do, a role to take, or a contribution to make. One assignment may seem more spectacular than another, but all are necessary to carry out God's greater plans for his church and for his world (12:12–27). Be available to God by placing your gifts at his service. Then as you discover what he calls you to do, be ready to do it.

- **1:1** Sosthenes may have been Paul's secretary who wrote down this letter as Paul dictated it. He was probably the Jewish synagogue leader in Corinth (Acts 18:17) who had been beaten during an attack on Paul, and then later became a believer. Sosthenes was well known to the members of the Corinthian church, and so Paul included his familiar name in the opening of the letter.

1:2 Corinth, a giant cultural melting pot with a great diversity of wealth, religions, and moral standards, had a reputation for being fiercely independent and as decadent as any city in the world. The

Romans had destroyed Corinth in 146 B.C. after a rebellion. But in 46 B.C., the Roman Emperor Julius Caesar rebuilt it because of its strategic seaport. By Paul's day (A.D. 50), the Romans had made Corinth the capital of Achaia (present-day Greece). It was a large city, offering Rome great profits through trade as well as the military protection of its ports. But the city's prosperity made it ripe for all sorts of corruption. Idolatry flourished, and there were more than a dozen pagan temples employing at least a thousand prostitutes. Corinth's reputation was such that prostitutes in other cities began to be called "Corinthian girls."

- **1:2** A personal invitation makes a person feel wanted and welcome. We are "called to be holy." God personally invites us to be citizens of his eternal kingdom. But Jesus Christ, God's Son, is the only one who can bring us into this glorious kingdom because he is the only one who removes our sins. *Sanctified* means that we are chosen or set apart by Christ for his service. We accept God's invitation by accepting his Son, Jesus Christ, and by trusting in the work he did on the cross to forgive our sins.

1:2 By including a salutation to "all those everywhere who call on the name of our Lord Jesus Christ," Paul is making it clear that this is not a private letter. Although it deals with specific issues facing the church at Corinth, all believers can learn from it. The Corinthian church included a great cross section of believers — wealthy merchants, common laborers, former temple prostitutes, and middle-class families. Because of the wide diversity of people and backgrounds, Paul takes great pains to stress the need for both spiritual unity and Christlike character.

to be holy, together with all those everywhere who call on the name of our Lord Jesus Christ — their Lord and ours:

³Grace and peace to you from God our Father and the Lord Jesus Christ. *d*

1:3
d Ro 1:7

Thanksgiving

⁴I always thank God for you *e* because of his grace given you in Christ Jesus. ⁵For in him you have been enriched in every way — in all your speaking and in all your knowledge — ⁶because our testimony *f* about Christ was confirmed in you. ⁷Therefore you do not lack any spiritual gift as you eagerly wait for our Lord Jesus Christ to be revealed. *g* ⁸He will keep you strong to the end, so that you will be blameless on the day of our Lord Jesus Christ. ⁹God, who has called you into fellowship with his Son Jesus Christ our Lord, is faithful. *h*

1:4
e Ro 1:8

1:6
f Rev 1:2

1:7
g 2Pe 3:12

1:9
h Isa 49:7

1. Divisions in the church

¹⁰I appeal to you, brothers, in the name of our Lord Jesus Christ, that all of you agree with one another so that there may be no divisions among you and that you may be perfectly united in mind and thought. ¹¹My brothers, some from Chloe's household have informed me that there are quarrels among you. ¹²What I mean is this: One of you says, "I follow Paul"; another, "I follow Apollos"; another, "I follow Cephas *a* "; still another, "I follow Christ."

¹³Is Christ divided? Was Paul crucified for you? Were you baptized into *b* the name of Paul? ¹⁴I am thankful that I did not baptize any of you except Crispus *i* and Gaius, *j* ¹⁵so no one can say that you were baptized into my name. ¹⁶(Yes, I also

1:14
i Ac 18:8
j Ac 19:29

a 12 That is, Peter　　**b** *13* Or *in*; also in verse 15

●**1:3** Grace is God's free gift of salvation given to us in Christ. Receiving it brings us peace (see Romans 5:1). In a world of noise, confusion, and relentless pressures, people long for peace. Many give up the search, thinking it impossible to find, but true peace of heart and mind is available to us through faith in Jesus Christ.

1:4–6 In this letter, Paul wrote some strong words to the Corinthians, but he began on a positive note of thanksgiving. He affirmed their privilege of belonging to the Lord and receiving his grace, the power God gave them to speak out for him and understand his truth, and the reality of their spiritual gifts. When we must correct others, it helps to begin by affirming what God has already accomplished in them.

●**1:7** The Corinthian church members had all the spiritual gifts they needed to live the Christian life, to witness for Christ, and to stand against the paganism and immorality of Corinth. But instead of using what God had given them, they were arguing over which gifts were more important. Paul addresses this issue in depth in chapters 12 – 14.

●**1:7–9** Paul guaranteed the Corinthian believers that God would consider them "blameless" when Christ returns (see Ephesians 1:7–10). This guarantee was not because of their great gifts or their shining performance, but because of what Jesus Christ accomplished for them through his death and resurrection. All who believe in the Lord Jesus will be considered blameless when Jesus Christ returns (see also 1 Thessalonians 3:13; Hebrews 9:28). If you have faith in Christ, even if it is weak, you are and will be saved.

1:10 Paul founded the church in Corinth on his second missionary journey. Eighteen months after he left, arguments and divisions arose, and some church members slipped back into an immoral life-style. Paul wrote this letter to address the problems, to clear up confusion about right and wrong, and to remove the immorality among them. The Corinthian people had a reputation for jumping from fad to fad; Paul wanted to keep Christianity from degenerating into just another fad.

1:10 By saying "brothers," Paul is emphasizing that all Christians are part of God's family. Believers share a unity that runs even deeper than that of blood brothers and sisters.

1:10, 11 To "agree with one another," allow for "no divisions" and "be perfectly united in mind and thought" does not require everyone to believe exactly the same. There is a difference between having opposing viewpoints and being divisive. A group of people will not completely agree on every issue, but they can work together harmoniously if they agree on what truly matters — Jesus Christ is Lord of all. In your church, speak and behave in a way that will reduce arguments and increase harmony. Petty differences should never divide Christians.

1:12ff In this large and diverse Corinthian church, the believers favored different preachers. Because there was as yet no written New Testament, the believers depended heavily on preaching and teaching for spiritual insight into the meaning of the Old Testament. Some followed Paul, who had founded their church; some who had heard Peter (Cephas) in Jerusalem followed him; while others listened only to Apollos, an eloquent and popular preacher who had had a dynamic ministry in Corinth (Acts 18:24; 19:1). Although these three preachers were united in their message, their personalities attracted different people. At this time the church was in danger of dividing. By mentioning Jesus Christ ten times in the first ten verses, Paul makes it clear who it is all preachers and teachers should emphasize. God's message is much more important than any human messenger.

1:12, 13 Paul wondered whether the Corinthians' quarrels had "divided" Christ. This is a graphic picture of what happens when the church (the body of Christ) is divided. With the many churches and styles of worship available today, we could get caught up in the same game of "my preacher is better than yours!" To do so would divide Christ again. But Christ is not divided, and his true followers should not allow anything to divide them. Don't let your appreciation for any teacher, preacher, or author lead you into intellectual pride. Our allegiance must be to Christ and to the unity that he desires.

1:16
k1Co 16:15

baptized the household of Stephanas;k beyond that, I don't remember if I baptized anyone else.) 17For Christ did not send me to baptize, but to preach the gospel — not with words of human wisdom, lest the cross of Christ be emptied of its power.

Christ the Wisdom and Power of God

1:18
lRo 1:16

18For the message of the cross is foolishness to those who are perishing, but to us who are being saved it is the power of God.l 19For it is written:

1:19
mIsa 29:14

"I will destroy the wisdom of the wise;
    the intelligence of the intelligent I will frustrate."cm

1:20
nRo 1:22

20Where is the wise man? Where is the scholar? Where is the philosopher of this age? Has not God made foolishn the wisdom of the world? 21For since in the wisdom of God the world through its wisdom did not know him, God was pleased through the foolishness of what was preached to save those who believe. 22Jews demand miraculous signso and Greeks look for wisdom, 23but we preach Christ crucified: a stumbling block to Jews and foolishness to Gentiles, 24but to those whom God has called, both Jews and Greeks, Christ the power of God and the wisdom of God.p 25For the foolishness of God is wiser than man's wisdom, and the weakness of God is stronger than man's strength.

1:22
oMt 12:38

1:24
pCol 2:3

c 19 Isaiah 29:14

HIGHLIGHTS OF 1 CORINTHIANS

The Meaning of the Cross 1:18—2:16	Be considerate of one another because of what Christ has done for us. There is no place for pride or a know-it-all attitude. We are to have the mind of Christ.
The Story of the Last Supper 11:23–29	The Last Supper is a time of reflection on Christ's final words to his disciples before he died on the cross; we must celebrate this in an orderly and correct manner.
The Poem of Love 13:1–13	Love is to guide all we do. We have different gifts, abilities, likes, dislikes—but we are called, without exception, to love.
The Christian's Destiny 15:42–58	We are promised by Christ, who died for us, that, as he came back to life after death, so our perishable bodies will be exchanged for heavenly bodies. Then we will live and reign with Christ.

1:17 When Paul said that Christ didn't send him to baptize, he wasn't minimizing the importance of baptism. Baptism was commanded by Jesus himself (Matthew 28:19) and practiced by the early church (Acts 2:41). Paul was emphasizing that no one person should do everything. Paul's gift was preaching, and that's what he did. Christian ministry should be a team effort; no preacher or teacher is a complete link between God and people, and no individual can do all that the apostles did. We must be content with the contribution God has given us to make, and carry it out wholeheartedly. (For more on different gifts, see chapters 12 and 13.)

1:17 Some speakers use impressive words, but they are weak on content. Paul stressed solid content and practical help for his listeners. He wanted them to be impressed with his *message*, not just his style (see 2:1–5). You don't need to be a great speaker with a large vocabulary to share the gospel effectively. The persuasive power is in the story, not the storyteller. Paul was not against those who carefully prepare what they say (see 2:6), but against those who try to impress others only with their own knowledge or speaking ability.

●**1:19** Paul summarizes Isaiah 29:14 to emphasize a point Jesus often made: God's way of thinking is not like the world's way (normal human wisdom). And God offers eternal life, which the world can never give. We can spend a lifetime accumulating human wisdom and yet never learn how to have a personal relationship with God. We must come to the crucified and risen Christ to receive eternal life and the joy of a personal relationship with our Savior.

●**1:22-24** Many Jews considered the Good News of Jesus Christ to be foolish, because they thought the Messiah would be a conquering king accompanied by signs and miracles. Jesus had not restored David's throne as they expected. Besides, he was executed as a criminal, and how could a criminal be a savior? Greeks, too, considered the gospel foolish: they did not believe in a bodily resurrection; they did not see in Jesus the powerful characteristics of their mythological gods; and they thought no reputable person would be crucified. To them, death was defeat, not victory.

The Good News of Jesus Christ still sounds foolish to many. Our society worships power, influence, and wealth. Jesus came as a humble, poor servant, and he offers his kingdom to those who have faith, not to those who do all kinds of good deeds to try to earn his gifts. This looks foolish to the world, but Christ is our power, the only way we can be saved. Knowing Christ personally is the greatest wisdom anyone could have.

●**1:25** The message of Christ's death for sins sounds foolish to those who don't believe. Death seems to be the end of the road, the ultimate weakness. But Jesus did not stay dead. His resurrection demonstrated his power even over death. And he will save us from eternal death and give us everlasting life if we trust him as Savior and Lord. This sounds so simple that many people won't accept it. They try other ways to obtain eternal life (being good, being wise, etc.). But all their attempts will not work. The "foolish" people who simply accept Christ's offer are actually the wisest of all, because they alone will live eternally with God.

26Brothers, think of what you were when you were called. Not many of you were wise by human standards; not many were influential; not many were of noble birth. 27But God chose*q* the foolish things of the world to shame the wise; God chose the weak things of the world to shame the strong. 28He chose the lowly things of this world and the despised things — and the things that are not — to nullify the things that are, 29so that no one may boast before him.*r* 30It is because of him that you are in Christ Jesus, who has become for us wisdom from God — that is, our righteousness, holiness and redemption. 31Therefore, as it is written: "Let him who boasts boast in the Lord."*d s*

2 When I came to you, brothers, I did not come with eloquence or superior wisdom*t* as I proclaimed to you the testimony about God.*e* 2For I resolved to know nothing while I was with you except Jesus Christ and him crucified.*u* 3I came to you in weakness and fear, and with much trembling. 4My message and my preaching were not with wise and persuasive words, but with a demonstration of the Spirit's power, 5so that your faith might not rest on men's wisdom, but on God's power.*v*

Wisdom From the Spirit

6We do, however, speak a message of wisdom among the mature, but not the wisdom of this age*w* or of the rulers of this age, who are coming to nothing. 7No, we speak of God's secret wisdom, a wisdom that has been hidden and that God destined for our glory before time began. 8None of the rulers of this age understood it, for if they had, they would not have crucified the Lord of glory. 9However, as it is written:

> "No eye has seen,
>   no ear has heard,
>   no mind has conceived
>   what God has prepared for those who love him"*f x* —

10but God has revealed it to us by his Spirit.

d 31 Jer. 9:24   *e* 1 Some manuscripts *as I proclaimed to you God's mystery*   *f* 9 Isaiah 64:4

1:27
q Jas 2:5

1:29
r Eph 2:9

1:31
s Jer 9:23, 24

2:1
t 1Co 1:17

2:2
u Gal 6:14

2:5
v 2Co 4:7

2:6
w 1Co 1:20

2:9
x Isa 64:4

1:27 Is Christianity against rational thinking? Christians clearly do believe in using their minds to weigh the evidence and make wise choices. Paul is declaring that no amount of human knowledge can replace or bypass Christ's work on the cross. If it could, Christ would be accessible only to the intellectually gifted and well educated, and not to ordinary people or to children.

1:28–31 Paul continues to emphasize that the way to receive salvation is so simple that *any* person who wants to can understand it. Skill and wisdom do not get a person into God's kingdom — simple faith does — so no one can boast that his or her achievements helped him or her secure eternal life. Salvation is totally from God through Jesus' death. There is *nothing* we can do to earn our salvation; we need only accept what Jesus has already done for us.

1:30 God is the source of and the reason for our personal and living relationship with Christ. Our union and identification with Christ results in our having God's wisdom and knowledge (Colossians 2:3), possessing right standing with God (*righteousness*, 2 Corinthians 5:21), being holy (1 Thessalonians 4:3–7), and having the penalty for our sins paid by Jesus (*redemption*, Mark 10:45).

2:1 Paul is referring to his first visit to Corinth during his second missionary journey (A.D. 51), when he founded the church (Acts 18:1ff).

2:1–5 A brilliant scholar, Paul could have overwhelmed his listeners with intellectual arguments. Instead he shared the simple message of Jesus Christ by allowing the Holy Spirit to guide his words. In sharing the gospel with others, we should follow Paul's example and keep our message simple and basic. The Holy Spirit will give power to our words and use them to bring glory to Jesus.

● **2:4** Paul's confidence was not in his keen intellect or speaking ability but in his knowledge that the Holy Spirit was helping and guiding him. Paul is not denying the importance of study and preparation for preaching — he had a thorough education in the Scriptures. Effective preaching must combine studious preparation with reliance on the work of the Holy Spirit. Don't use Paul's statement as an excuse for not studying or preparing.

● **2:7** God's "secret wisdom . . . that has been hidden" was his offer of salvation to all people. Originally unknown to humanity, this plan became crystal clear when Jesus rose from the dead. His resurrection proved that he had power over sin and death and could offer us this power as well (see also 1 Peter 1:10–12 and the first note on Romans 16:25–27). God's plan, however, is still hidden to unbelievers because they either refuse to accept it, choose to ignore it, or simply haven't heard about it.

2:8 Jesus was misunderstood and rejected by those whom the world considered wise and great. He was put to death by the rulers in Palestine — the high priest, King Herod, Pilate, and the Pharisees and Sadducees. Jesus' rejection by these rulers had been predicted in Isaiah 53:3 and Zechariah 12:10, 11.

2:9 We cannot imagine all that God has in store for us, both in this life and for eternity. He will create a new heaven and a new earth (Isaiah 65:17; Revelation 21:1), and we will live with him forever. Until then, his Holy Spirit comforts and guides us. Knowing the wonderful and eternal future that awaits us gives us hope and courage to press on in this life, to endure hardship, and to avoid giving in to temptation. This world is not all there is. The best is yet to come.

● **2:10** The "deep things of God" refers to God's unfathomable nature and his wonderful plan — Jesus' death and resurrection — and to the promise of salvation, revealed only to those who believe that

2:11
y Pr 20:27

2:12
z Ro 8:15

2:14
a 1Co 1:18

2:16
b Jn 15:15

3:1
c 1Co 2:15
d 1Co 2:14

3:2
e Heb 5:12-14;
1Pe 2:2

3:3
f Gal 5:20

3:6
g Ac 18:4-11

3:9
h 2Co 6:1
i Eph 2:20-22

The Spirit searches all things, even the deep things of God. [11]For who among men knows the thoughts of a man except the man's spirit[y] within him? In the same way no one knows the thoughts of God except the Spirit of God. [12]We have not received the spirit[z] of the world but the Spirit who is from God, that we may understand what God has freely given us. [13]This is what we speak, not in words taught us by human wisdom but in words taught by the Spirit, expressing spiritual truths in spiritual words.[g] [14]The man without the Spirit does not accept the things that come from the Spirit of God, for they are foolishness[a] to him, and he cannot understand them, because they are spiritually discerned. [15]The spiritual man makes judgments about all things, but he himself is not subject to any man's judgment:

[16]"For who has known the mind of the Lord
    that he may instruct him?"[h]

But we have the mind of Christ. [b]

On Divisions in the Church

3 Brothers, I could not address you as spiritual[c] but as worldly[d] — mere infants in Christ. [2]I gave you milk, not solid food,[e] for you were not yet ready for it. Indeed, you are still not ready. [3]You are still worldly. For since there is jealousy and quarreling[f] among you, are you not worldly? Are you not acting like mere men? [4]For when one says, "I follow Paul," and another, "I follow Apollos," are you not mere men?

[5]What, after all, is Apollos? And what is Paul? Only servants, through whom you came to believe — as the Lord has assigned to each his task. [6]I planted the seed,[g] Apollos watered it, but God made it grow. [7]So neither he who plants nor he who waters is anything, but only God, who makes things grow. [8]The man who plants and the man who waters have one purpose, and each will be rewarded according to his own labor. [9]For we are God's fellow workers;[h] you are God's field, God's building. [i]

g 13 Or *Spirit, interpreting spiritual truths to spiritual men*   **h** 16 Isaiah 40:13

---

what God says is true. Those who believe in Christ's death and resurrection and put their faith in him will know all they need to know to be saved. This knowledge, however, can't be grasped by even the wisest people unless they accept God's message. All who reject God's message are foolish, no matter how wise the world thinks they are.

2:13 Paul's words are authoritative because their source was the Holy Spirit. Paul was not merely giving his own personal views or his personal impression of what God had said. Under the inspiration of the Holy Spirit, he wrote the very thoughts and words of God.

● **2:14, 15** Non-Christians cannot understand God, and they cannot grasp the concept that God's Spirit lives in believers. Don't expect most people to approve of or understand your decision to follow Christ. It all seems so silly to them. Just as a tone-deaf person cannot appreciate fine music, the person who rejects God cannot understand God's beautiful message. With the lines of communication broken, he or she won't be able to hear what God is saying to him or her.

2:15, 16 No one can comprehend God (Romans 11:34), but through the guidance of the Holy Spirit, believers have insight into some of God's plans, thoughts, and actions — they, in fact, have the "mind of Christ." Through the Holy Spirit we can begin to know God's thoughts, talk with him, and expect his answers to our prayers. Are you spending enough time with Christ to have his very mind in you? An intimate relationship with Christ comes only from spending time consistently in his presence and in his Word. Read Philippians 2:5ff for more on the mind of Christ.

3:1-3 Paul called the Corinthians infants in the Christian life because they were not yet spiritually healthy and mature. The proof was that they quarreled like children, allowing divisions to distract them. Immature Christians are "worldly," controlled by their own desires; mature believers are in tune with God's desires. How much influence do your desires have on your life? Your goal should be to let God's desires be yours. Being controlled by your own desires will stunt your growth.

●**3:6** Paul planted the seed of the gospel message in people's hearts. He was a missionary pioneer; he brought the message of salvation. Apollos's role was to water — to help the believers grow stronger in the faith. Paul founded the church in Corinth, and Apollos built on that foundation. Tragically, the believers in Corinth had split into factions, pledging loyalty to different teachers (see 1:11-13). After the preachers' work is completed, God keeps on making Christians grow. Our leaders should certainly be respected, but we should never place them on pedestals that create barriers between people or set them up as a substitute for Christ.

3:7-9 God's work involves many different individuals with a variety of gifts and abilities. There are no superstars in this task, only team members performing their own special roles. We can become useful members of God's team by setting aside our desires to receive glory for what we do. Don't seek the praise that comes from people — it is comparatively worthless. Instead, seek approval from God.

10By the grace God has given me,*j* I laid a foundation as an expert builder, and someone else is building on it. But each one should be careful how he builds. 11For no one can lay any foundation other than the one already laid, which is Jesus Christ.*k* 12If any man builds on this foundation using gold, silver, costly stones, wood, hay or straw, 13his work will be shown for what it is, because the Day*l* will bring it to light. It will be revealed with fire, and the fire will test the quality of each man's work. 14If what he has built survives, he will receive his reward. 15If it is burned up, he will suffer loss; he himself will be saved, but only as one escaping through the flames.*m*

16Don't you know that you yourselves are God's temple*n* and that God's Spirit lives in you? 17If anyone destroys God's temple, God will destroy him; for God's temple is sacred, and you are that temple.

18Do not deceive yourselves. If any one of you thinks he is wise by the standards of this age, he should become a "fool" so that he may become wise. 19For the wisdom of this world is foolishness in God's sight. As it is written: "He catches the wise in their craftiness"*i;o* 20and again, "The Lord knows that the thoughts of the wise are futile."*jp* 21So then, no more boasting about men! All things are yours,*q* 22whether Paul or Apollos or Cephas*k* or the world or life or death or the present or the future — all are yours, 23and you are of Christ,*r* and Christ is of God.

Apostles of Christ

4 So then, men ought to regard us as servants of Christ and as those entrusted with the secret things of God. 2Now it is required that those who have been given a trust must prove faithful. 3I care very little if I am judged by you or by any human court; indeed, I do not even judge myself. 4My conscience is clear, but that does not make me innocent.*s* It is the Lord who judges me. 5Therefore judge nothing before the appointed time; wait till the Lord comes. He will bring to light what

i 19 Job 5:13   *j 20* Psalm 94:11   *k 22* That is, Peter

3:10
j Ro 12:3

3:11
k Eph 2:20

3:13
l 2Th 1:7-10

3:15
m Jude 23

3:16
n 2Co 6:16

3:19
o Job 5:13

3:20
p Ps 94:11

3:21
q Ro 8:32

3:23
r 2Co 10:7;
Gal 3:29

4:4
s Ro 2:13

●**3:10, 11** The foundation of the church — of all believers — is Jesus Christ. Paul laid this foundation (by preaching Christ) when he began the church at Corinth. Whoever builds the church — officers, teachers, preachers, parents, and others — must build with high-quality materials (right doctrine and right living, 3:12ff) that meet God's standards. Paul is not criticizing Apollos, but challenging future church leaders to have sound preaching and teaching.

●**3:10-17** In the church built on Jesus Christ, each church member would be mature, spiritually sensitive, and doctrinally sound. However, the Corinthian church was filled with those whose work was "wood, hay, straw," members who were immature, insensitive to one another, and vulnerable to wrong doctrine (3:1-4). No wonder they had so many problems. Local church members should be deeply committed to Christ. Can your Christian character stand the test?

3:11 A building is only as solid as its foundation. The foundation of our lives is Jesus Christ; he is our base, our reason for being. Everything we are and do must fit into the pattern provided by him. Are you building your life on the only real and lasting foundation, or are you building on a faulty foundation such as wealth, security, success, or fame?

●**3:13-15** Two sure ways to destroy a building are to tamper with the foundation and to build with inferior materials. The church must be built on Christ, not on any other person or principle. Christ will evaluate each minister's contribution to the life of the church, and the day of judgment ("the Day") will reveal the sincerity of each person's work. God will determine whether or not they have been faithful to Jesus' instructions. Good work will be rewarded; unfaithful or inferior work will be discounted. The builder "will be saved, but only as one escaping through the flames" means that unfaithful workers will be saved, but like people escaping from a burning building. All their possessions (accomplishments) will be lost.

3:16, 17 Just as our bodies are the "temple of the Holy Spirit" (6:19), the local church or Christian community is God's temple. Just as the Jews' temple in Jerusalem was not to be destroyed, the church is not to be spoiled and ruined by divisions, controversy, or other sins as members come together to worship God.

3:18-21 Paul was not telling the Corinthian believers to neglect the pursuit of knowledge. He was warning them that if worldly wisdom holds them back from God, it is not wisdom at all. God's way of thinking is far more valuable, even though it may seem foolish to the world (1:27). The Corinthians were using so-called worldly wisdom to evaluate their leaders and teachers. Their pride made them value the presentation of the message more than its content.

3:22 Paul says that both life and death are ours. While nonbelievers are swept along by its current and wondering if there is meaning to it, believers can use life well because they understand its true purpose. Nonbelievers can only fear death. For believers, however, death holds no terrors because Christ has conquered all fears (see 1 John 4:18). Death is only the beginning of eternal life with God.

●**4:1, 2** Paul urged the Corinthians to think of him, Peter (Cephas), and Apollos not as leaders of factions, but as servants of Christ entrusted with the secret things of God (see the note on 2:7). A servant does what his master tells him to do. We must do what God tells us to do in the Bible and through his Holy Spirit. Each day God presents us with needs and opportunities that challenge us to do what we know is right.

4:5 It is tempting to judge fellow Christians, evaluating whether or not they are good followers of Christ. But only God knows a person's heart, and he is the only one with the right to judge. Paul's warning to the Corinthians should also warn us. We are to confront those who are sinning (see 5:12, 13), but we must not judge who is a better servant for Christ. When you judge someone, you invariably consider yourself better — and that is arrogant.

is hidden in darkness and will expose the motives of men's hearts. At that time each will receive his praise from God. [t]

6Now, brothers, I have applied these things to myself and Apollos for your benefit, so that you may learn from us the meaning of the saying, "Do not go beyond what is written." Then you will not take pride in one man over against another. [u] 7For who makes you different from anyone else? What do you have that you did not receive? And if you did receive it, why do you boast as though you did not?

4:6
[u] 1Co 1:12

8Already you have all you want! Already you have become rich! [v] You have become kings — and that without us! How I wish that you really had become kings so that we might be kings with you! 9For it seems to me that God has put us apostles on display at the end of the procession, like men condemned to die in the arena. We have been made a spectacle [w] to the whole universe, to angels as well as to men. 10We are fools for Christ, [x] but you are so wise in Christ! We are weak, but you are strong! You are honored, we are dishonored! 11To this very hour we go hungry and thirsty, we are in rags, we are brutally treated, we are homeless. [y] 12We work hard with our own hands. [z] When we are cursed, we bless; when we are persecuted, we endure it; 13when we are slandered, we answer kindly. Up to this moment we have become the scum of the earth, the refuse of the world.

4:8
[v] Rev 3:17, 18

4:9
[w] Heb 10:33

4:10
[x] Ac 17:18

4:11
[y] Ro 8:35

4:12
[z] Ac 18:3

14I am not writing this to shame you, but to warn you, as my dear children. [a] 15Even though you have ten thousand guardians in Christ, you do not have many fathers, for in Christ Jesus I became your father through the gospel. 16Therefore I urge you to imitate me. [b] 17For this reason I am sending to you Timothy, my son whom I love, who is faithful in the Lord. He will remind you of my way of life in Christ Jesus, which agrees with what I teach everywhere in every church. [c]

4:14
[a] 1Th 2:11

4:16
[b] 1Th 1:6

4:17
[c] 1Co 7:17

18Some of you have become arrogant, as if I were not coming to you. 19But I will come to you very soon, [d] if the Lord is willing, and then I will find out not only how these arrogant people are talking, but what power they have. 20For the kingdom of God is not a matter of talk but of power. 21What do you prefer? Shall I come to you with a whip, [e] or in love and with a gentle spirit?

4:19
[d] 2Co 1:15, 16

4:21
[e] 2Co 1:23; 13:2, 10

●4:6, 7 How easy it is for us to become attached to a spiritual leader. When someone has helped us, it's natural to feel loyalty. But Paul warns against having such pride in our favorite leaders that we cause divisions in the church. Any true spiritual leader is a representative of Christ and has nothing to offer that God hasn't given him or her. Don't let your loyalty cause strife, slander, or broken relationships. Make sure that your deepest loyalties are to Christ and not to his human agents. Those who spend more time debating church leadership than declaring Christ's message don't have Christ as their top priority.

4:6–13 The Corinthians had split into various cliques, each following its favorite preacher (Paul, Apollos, Peter, etc.). Each clique really believed it was the only one to have the whole truth, and thus felt spiritually proud. But Paul told the groups not to boast about being tied to a particular preacher because each preacher was simply a humble servant who had suffered for the same message of salvation in Jesus Christ. No preacher of God has more status than another.

●4:15 In Paul's day, a guardian was a slave who was assigned as a special tutor and caretaker of a child. Paul was portraying his special affection for the Corinthians (greater than a slave) and his special role (more than a caretaker). In an attempt to unify the church, Paul appealed to his relationship with them. By father, he meant he was the church's founder. Because he started the church, he could be trusted to have its best interests at heart. Paul's tough words were motivated by love — like the love a good father has for his children (see also 1 Thessalonians 2:11).

4:16 Paul told the Corinthians to imitate him. He was able to make this statement because he walked close to God, spent time in God's Word and in prayer, and was aware of God's presence in his life at all times. God was Paul's example; therefore, Paul's life could be an example to other Christians. Paul wasn't expecting others to imitate everything he did, but they should imitate those aspects of his beliefs and conduct that were modeling Christ's way of living.

4:17 Timothy had traveled with Paul on Paul's second missionary journey (see Acts 16:1–3) and was a key person in the growth of the early church. Timothy may have delivered this letter to Corinth, but more likely he arrived there shortly after the letter came (see 16:10). Timothy's role was to see that Paul's advice was received, read, and implemented. Then he was to return to Paul and report on the church's progress.

4:18-20 Some people talk a lot about faith, but that's all it is — talk. They may know all the right words to say, but their lives don't reflect God's power. Paul says that the kingdom of God is to be lived, not just discussed. There is a big difference between knowing the right words and living them out. Don't be content to have the right answers about Christ. Let your life show that God's power is really working in you.

4:19 It is not known whether Paul ever returned to Corinth, but it is likely. In 2 Corinthians 2:1, he writes that he decided not to make "another painful visit," implying that he had had a previous painful confrontation with the Corinthian believers (see 2 Corinthians 12:14; 13:1; and the note on 2 Corinthians 2:1).

2. Disorder in the church

Expel the Immoral Brother!

5 It is actually reported that there is sexual immorality among you, and of a kind that does not occur even among pagans: A man has his father's wife.*f* 2And you are proud! Shouldn't you rather have been filled with grief*g* and have put out of your fellowship the man who did this? 3Even though I am not physically present, I am with you in spirit.*h* And I have already passed judgment on the one who did this, just as if I were present. 4When you are assembled in the name of our Lord Jesus and I am with you in spirit, and the power of our Lord Jesus is present, 5hand this man over*i* to Satan, so that the sinful nature*1* may be destroyed and his spirit saved on the day of the Lord.

6Your boasting is not good. Don't you know that a little yeast works through the whole batch of dough?*j* 7Get rid of the old yeast that you may be a new batch without yeast — as you really are. For Christ, our Passover lamb, has been sacrificed.*k* 8Therefore let us keep the Festival, not with the old yeast, the yeast of malice and wickedness, but with bread without yeast,*l* the bread of sincerity and truth.

9I have written you in my letter not to associate*m* with sexually immoral people — 10not at all meaning the people of this world*n* who are immoral, or the greedy and swindlers, or idolaters. In that case you would have to leave this world. 11But now I am writing you that you must not associate with anyone who calls himself a brother but is sexually immoral or greedy, an idolater or a slanderer, a drunkard or a swindler. With such a man do not even eat.

12What business is it of mine to judge those outside*o* the church? Are you not to judge those inside?*p* 13God will judge those outside. "Expel the wicked man from among you."*m q*

1 5 Or *that his body;* or *that the flesh* *m* 13 Deut. 17:7; 19:19; 21:21; 22:21,24; 24:7

5:1
*f*Lev 18:8

5:2
*g*2Co 7:7-11

5:3
*h*Col 2:5

5:5
*i*1Ti 1:20

5:6
*j*Gal 5:9

5:7
*k*1Pe 1:19

5:8
*l*Dt 16:3

5:9
*m*Eph 5:11

5:10
*n*1Co 10:27

5:12
*o*Mk 4:11
*p*1Co 6:1-4

5:13
*q*Dt 13:5

●**5:1ff** The church must discipline flagrant sin among its members — such sins, left unchecked, can polarize and paralyze a church. The correction, however, should never be vengeful. Instead, it should be given to help bring about a cure. There was a specific sin in the church, but the Corinthian believers had refused to deal with it. In this case, a man was having an affair with his mother (or stepmother), and the church members were trying to ignore the situation. Paul was telling the church that it had a responsibility to maintain the standards of morality found in God's commandments. God tells us not to judge others. But he also tells us not to tolerate flagrant sin because leaving that sin undisciplined will have a dangerous influence on other believers (5:6).

●**5:5** To "hand this man over to Satan" means to exclude him from the fellowship of believers. Without the spiritual support of Christians, this man would be left alone with his sin and Satan, and perhaps this emptiness would drive him to repentance. "That the sinful nature may be destroyed" states the hope that the experience would bring him to God to destroy his sinful nature through repentance. *Sinful nature* could mean his body or flesh (see the NIV text note). This alternative translation would imply that Satan would afflict him physically and thus bring him to God. Putting someone out of the church should be a last resort in disciplinary action. It should not be done out of vengeance, but out of love, just as parents punish children to correct and restore them. The church's role should be to help, not hurt, offenders, motivating them to repent of their sins and to return to the fellowship of the church.

●**5:6** Paul was writing to those who wanted to ignore this church problem. They didn't realize that allowing public sin to exist in the church affects all its members. Paul does not expect anyone to be sinless — all believers struggle with sin daily. Instead, he is speaking against those who deliberately sin, feel no guilt, and refuse to repent. This kind of sin cannot be tolerated in the church because it affects others. We have a responsibility to other believers. Yeast makes bread dough rise. A little bit affects the whole batch. Blatant

sins, left uncorrected, confuse and divide the congregation. While believers should encourage, pray for, and build up one another, they must also be intolerant of sin that jeopardizes the spiritual health of the church.

5:7, 8 As the Hebrews prepared for their exodus from slavery in Egypt, they were commanded to prepare bread without yeast because they didn't have time to wait for it to rise. And because yeast also was a symbol of sin, they were commanded to sweep all of it out of the house (Exodus 12:15; 13:7). Christ is our Passover lamb, the perfect sacrifice for our sin. Because he has delivered us from the slavery of sin, we should have nothing to do with the sins of the past ("old yeast").

5:9 Paul is referring to an earlier letter to the Corinthian church, often called the lost letter because it has not been preserved.

●**5:10, 11** Paul makes it clear that we should not disassociate ourselves from unbelievers — otherwise, we could not carry out Christ's command to tell them about salvation (Matthew 28:18–20). But we are to distance ourselves from the person who claims to be a Christian, yet indulges in sins explicitly forbidden in Scripture and then rationalizes his or her actions. By rationalizing sin, a person harms others for whom Christ died and dims the image of God in himself or herself. A church that includes such people is hardly fit to be the light of the world. To do so would distort the picture of Christ it presents to the world. Church leaders must be ready to correct, in love, for the sake of spiritual unity.

●**5:12** The Bible consistently tells us not to criticize people by gossiping or making rash judgments. At the same time, however, we are to judge and deal with sin that can hurt others. Paul's instructions should not be used to handle trivial matters or to take revenge; nor should they be applied to individual problems between believers. These verses are instructions for dealing with open sin in the church, with a person who claims to be a Christian and yet who sins without remorse. The church is to confront and discipline such a person in love. Also see the notes on 4:5 and 5:1ff.

Lawsuits Among Believers

6 If any of you has a dispute with another, dare he take it before the ungodly for judgment instead of before the saints? 2Do you not know that the saints will judge the world?ʳ And if you are to judge the world, are you not competent to judge trivial cases? 3Do you not know that we will judge angels? How much more the things of this life! 4Therefore, if you have disputes about such matters, appoint as judges even men of little account in the church!ⁿ 5I say this to shame you. Is it possible that there is nobody among you wise enough to judge a dispute between believers? 6But instead, one brother goes to law against another — and this in front of unbelievers!

7The very fact that you have lawsuits among you means you have been completely defeated already. Why not rather be wronged? Why not rather be cheated?ˢ 8Instead, you yourselves cheat and do wrong, and you do this to your brothers.ᵗ

9Do you not know that the wicked will not inherit the kingdom of God? Do not be deceived: Neither the sexually immoral nor idolaters nor adulterers nor male prostitutes nor homosexual offenders 10nor thieves nor the greedy nor drunkards nor slanderers nor swindlers will inherit the kingdom of God. 11And that is what some of you were. But you were washed, you were sanctified, you were justified in the name of the Lord Jesus Christ and by the Spirit of our God.

n 4 Or matters, do you appoint as judges men of little account in the church?

6:2 ʳMt 19:28

6:7 ˢMt 5:39, 40

6:8 ᵗ1Th 4:6

✶ **CHURCH DISCIPLINE**
The church, at times, must exercise discipline toward members who have sinned. But church discipline must be handled carefully, straightforwardly, and lovingly.

Situations
Unintentional error and/or private sin
Public sin and/or those done flagrantly and arrogantly

Steps (Matthew 18:15–17)
1. Go to the brother or sister, show the fault to him or her in private.
2. If he/she does not listen, go with one or two witnesses.
3. If he/she refuses to listen, take the matter before the church.

After these steps have been carried out, the next steps are:
1. Remove the one in error from the fellowship (1 Corinthians 5:2–13).
2. The church gives united disapproval, but forgiveness and comfort are in order if he/she chooses to repent (2 Corinthians 2:5–8).
3. Do not associate with the disobedient person; and if you must, speak to him/her as one who needs a warning (2 Thessalonians 3:14, 15).
4. After two warnings, reject the person from the fellowship (Titus 3:10).

●**6:1–6** In chapter 5, Paul explained what to do with open immorality in the congregation. In chapter 6, he teaches how the congregation should handle smaller problems between believers. Society has set up a legal system where disagreements can be resolved in courts. But Paul declares that disagreeing Christians should not have to go to a secular court to resolve their differences. As Christians, we have the Holy Spirit and the mind of Christ, so why should we turn to those who lack God's wisdom? Because of all that we have been given as believers, and because of the authority that we will have in the future to judge the world and the angels, we should be able to deal with disputes among ourselves. The *saints* are believers. See John 5:22 and Revelation 3:21 for more on judging the world. Judging angels is mentioned in 2 Peter 2:4 and Jude 6.

6:6–8 Why did Paul say that Christians should not take their disagreements to unbelievers in secular courts? (1) If the judge and jury are not Christians, they are not likely to be sensitive to Christian values. (2) The basis for going to court is often revenge; this should never be a Christian's motive. (3) Lawsuits make the church look bad, causing unbelievers to focus on its problems rather than on its purpose.

6:9–11 Paul is describing characteristics of unbelievers. He doesn't mean that idolaters, adulterers, male prostitutes, homosexuals, thieves, greedy people, drunkards, slanderers or swindlers are automatically and irrevocably excluded from heaven. Christians come out of all kinds of different backgrounds, including these. They may still struggle with evil desires, but they should not continue in these practices. In 6:11, Paul clearly states that even those who sin in these ways can have their lives changed by Christ. However, those who say that they are Christians but persist in these practices with no sign of remorse will not inherit the kingdom of God. Such people need to reevaluate their lives to see if they truly believe in Christ.

●**6:9–11** In a permissive society it is easy for Christians to overlook or tolerate some immoral behaviors (greed, drunkenness, etc.) while remaining outraged at others (homosexuality, thievery). We must not participate in sin or condone it in any way, nor may we be selective about what we condemn or excuse. Staying away from more "acceptable" forms of sin is difficult, but it is no harder for us than it was for the Corinthians. God expects his followers in any age to have high standards.

6:11 Paul emphasizes God's action in making believers new people. The three aspects of God's work are all part of our salvation: our sins were washed away, we were set apart for special use ("sanctified"), and we were pronounced not guilty ("justified") for our sins.

Sexual Immorality

12"Everything is permissible for me" — but not everything is beneficial. *u* "Everything is permissible for me" — but I will not be mastered by anything. 13"Food for the stomach and the stomach for food" — but God will destroy them both. The body is not meant for sexual immorality, but for the Lord, and the Lord for the body. 14By his power God raised the Lord from the dead, and he will raise us also. 15Do you not know that your bodies are members of Christ himself? *v* Shall I then take the members of Christ and unite them with a prostitute? Never! 16Do you not know that he who unites himself with a prostitute is one with her in body? For it is said, "The two will become one flesh." *o w* 17But he who unites himself with the Lord is one with him in spirit. *x*

18Flee from sexual immorality. *y* All other sins a man commits are outside his body, but he who sins sexually sins against his own body. *z* 19Do you not know that your body is a temple of the Holy Spirit, who is in you, whom you have received from God? You are not your own; *a* 20you were bought at a price. *b* Therefore honor God with your body.

o 16 Gen. 2:24

6:12
u 1Co 10:23

6:15
v Ro 12:5
6:16
w Ge 2:24;
Mt 19:5;
Eph 5:31
6:17
x Jn 17:21-23
6:18
y Heb 13:4
z Ro 6:12
6:19
a Ro 14:7, 8
6:20
b Rev 5:9

6:12 Apparently the church had been quoting and misapplying the words "everything is permissible for me." Some Christians in Corinth were excusing their sins by saying that (1) Christ had taken away all sin, and so they had complete freedom to live as they pleased, or (2) what they were doing was not strictly forbidden by Scripture. Paul answered both these excuses. (1) While Christ has taken away our sin, this does not give us freedom to go on doing what we know is wrong. The New Testament specifically forbids many sins (see 6:9, 10) that were originally prohibited in the Old Testament (see Romans 12:9–21; 13:8–10). (2) Some actions are not sinful in themselves, but they are not appropriate because they can control our lives and lead us away from God. (3) Some actions may hurt others. Anything we do that hurts rather than helps others is not right.

6:12, 13 Many of the world's religions teach that the soul or spirit is important but the body is not; and Christianity has sometimes been influenced by these ideas. In truth, however, Christianity takes very seriously the realm of the physical. We worship a God who created a physical world and pronounced it good. He promises us a new earth where real people have transformed physical lives — not a pink cloud where disembodied souls listen to harp music. At the heart of Christianity is the story of God himself taking on flesh and blood and coming to live with us, offering both physical healing and spiritual restoration.

We humans, like Adam, are a combination of dust and spirit. Just as our spirits affect our bodies, so our physical bodies affect our spirits. We cannot commit sin with our bodies without damaging our souls because our bodies and souls are inseparably joined. In the new earth we will have resurrection bodies that are not corrupted by sin. Then we will enjoy the fullness of our salvation.

●**6:12, 13** Freedom is a mark of the Christian faith — freedom from sin and guilt, and freedom to use and enjoy anything that comes

from God. But Christians should not abuse this freedom and hurt themselves or others. Drinking too much leads to alcoholism, gluttony leads to obesity. Be careful that what God has allowed you to enjoy doesn't grow into a bad habit that controls you. For more about Christian freedom and everyday behavior, read chapter 8.

●**6:13** Sexual immorality is a temptation that is always before us. In movies and on television, sex outside marriage is treated as a normal, even desirable, part of life, while marriage is often shown as confining and joyless. We can even be looked down on by others if we are suspected of being pure. But God does not forbid sexual sin just to be difficult. He knows its power to destroy us physically and spiritually. No one should underestimate the power of sexual immorality. It has devastated countless lives and destroyed families, churches, communities, and even nations. God wants to protect us from damaging ourselves and others, and so he offers to fill us — our loneliness, our desires — with himself.

6:15–17 This teaching about sexual immorality and prostitutes was especially important for the Corinthian church because the temple of the love goddess Aphrodite was in Corinth. This temple employed more than a thousand prostitutes as priestesses, and sex was part of the worship ritual. Paul clearly stated that Christians are to have no part in sexual immorality, even if it is acceptable and popular in our culture.

6:18 Christians are free to be all they can be for God, but they are not free *from* God. God created sex to be a beautiful and essential ingredient of marriage, but sexual sin — sex outside the marriage relationship — *always* hurts someone. It hurts God because it shows that we prefer following our own desires instead of the leading of the Holy Spirit. It hurts others because it violates the commitment so necessary to a relationship. It often brings disease to our bodies. And it deeply affects our personalities, which respond in anguish when we harm ourselves physically and spiritually.

●**6:19, 20** What did Paul mean when he said that our bodies belong to God? Many people say they have the right to do whatever they want with their own bodies. Although they think that this is freedom, they are really enslaved to their own desires. When we become Christians, the Holy Spirit fills and lives in us. Therefore, we no longer own our bodies. "Bought at a price" refers to slaves purchased at auction. Christ's death freed us from sin, but also obligates us to his service. If you live in a building owned by someone else, you try not to violate the building's rules. Because your body belongs to God, you must not violate his standards for living.

B. PAUL ANSWERS CHURCH QUESTIONS (7:1 — 16:24)

After discussing disorder in the church, Paul moves to the list of questions that the Corinthians had sent him, including subjects of marriage, singleness, eating meat offered to idols, propriety in worship, orderliness in the Lord's Supper, spiritual gifts, and the resurrection. Questions that plague churches today are remarkably similar to these, so we can receive specific guidance in these areas from the letter.

1. Instruction on Christian marriage

7:1
c ver 8, 26

7 Now for the matters you wrote about: It is good for a man not to marry.P c ²But since there is so much immorality, each man should have his own wife, and each woman her own husband. ³The husband should fulfill his marital duty to his wife, and likewise the wife to her husband. ⁴The wife's body does not belong to her alone but also to her husband. In the same way, the husband's body does not belong to him alone but also to his wife. ⁵Do not deprive each other except by mutual consent and for a time,ᵈ so that you may devote yourselves to prayer. Then come together again so that Satan will not tempt you because of your lack of self-control. ⁶I say this as a concession, not as a command.ᵉ ⁷I wish that all men were as I am.ᶠ But each man has his own gift from God; one has this gift, another has that.ᵍ

7:5
d Ex 19:15;
1Sa 21:4, 5

7:6
e 2Co 8:8

7:7
f 1Co 9:5
g 1Co 12:4, 11

⁸Now to the unmarried and the widows I say: It is good for them to stay unmarried, as I am.ʰ ⁹But if they cannot control themselves, they should marry,ⁱ for it is better to marry than to burn with passion.

7:8
h ver 1, 26

7:9
i 1Ti 5:14

¹⁰To the married I give this command (not I, but the Lord): A wife must not separate from her husband.ʲ ¹¹But if she does, she must remain unmarried or else be reconciled to her husband. And a husband must not divorce his wife.

7:10
j Mal 2:14-16;
Lk 16:18

p 1 Or "It is good for a man not to have sexual relations with a woman."

7:1 The Corinthians had written to Paul, asking him several questions relating to the Christian life and problems in the church. The first question was whether it was good to be married. Paul answers this and other questions in the remainder of this letter.

7:1ff Christians in Corinth were surrounded by sexual temptation. The city had a reputation even among pagans for sexual immorality and religious prostitution. It was to this kind of society that Paul delivered these instructions on sex and marriage. The Corinthians needed special, specific instructions because of their culture's immoral standards. For more on Paul's teaching about marriage, see Ephesians 5.

7:3-5 Sexual temptations are difficult to withstand because they appeal to the normal and natural desires that God has given us. Marriage provides God's way to satisfy these natural sexual desires and to strengthen the partners against temptation. Married couples have the responsibility to care for each other; therefore, husbands and wives should not withhold themselves sexually from one another, but should fulfill each other's needs and desires. (See also the note on 10:13.)

● **7:3-11** The Corinthian church was in turmoil because of the immorality of the culture around them. Some Greeks, in rejecting immorality, rejected sex and marriage altogether. The Corinthian Christians wondered if this was what they should do also, so they asked Paul several questions: "Because sex is perverted, shouldn't we also abstain in marriage?" "If my spouse is unsaved, should I seek a divorce?" "Should unmarried people and widows remain unmarried?" Paul answered many of these questions by saying, "For now, stay put. Be content in the situation where God has placed you. If you're married, don't seek to be single. If you're single, don't seek to be married. Live God's way, one day at a time, and he will show you what to do."

● **7:4** Spiritually, our bodies belong to God when we become Christians because Jesus Christ bought us by paying the price to re-

lease us from sin (see 6:19, 20). Physically, our bodies belong to our spouses because God designed marriage so that, through the union of husband and wife, the two become one (Genesis 2:24). Paul stressed complete equality in sexual relationships. Neither male nor female should seek dominance or autonomy.

● **7:7** Both marriage and singleness are gifts from God. One is not morally better than the other, and both are valuable to accomplishing God's purposes. It is important for us, therefore, to accept our present situation. When Paul said he wished that all people were like him (i.e., unmarried), he was expressing his desire that more people would devote themselves *completely* to the ministry without the added concerns of spouse and family, as he had done. He was not criticizing marriage — after all, it is God's created way of providing companionship and populating the earth.

7:9 Sexual pressure is not the best motive for getting married, but it is better to marry the right person than to "burn with passion." Many new believers in Corinth thought that all sex was wrong, and so engaged couples were deciding not to get married. In this passage, Paul was telling couples who wanted to marry that they should not frustrate their normal sexual drives by avoiding marriage. This does not mean, however, that people who have trouble controlling themselves should marry the first person who comes along. It is better to deal with the pressure of desire than to deal with an unhappy marriage.

12To the rest I say this (I, not the Lord): If any brother has a wife who is not a believer and she is willing to live with him, he must not divorce her. 13And if a woman has a husband who is not a believer and he is willing to live with her, she must not divorce him. 14For the unbelieving husband has been sanctified through his wife, and the unbelieving wife has been sanctified through her believing husband. Otherwise your children would be unclean, but as it is, they are holy.*k*

15But if the unbeliever leaves, let him do so. A believing man or woman is not bound in such circumstances; God has called us to live in peace.*l* 16How do you know, wife, whether you will save your husband?*m* Or, how do you know, husband, whether you will save your wife?

17Nevertheless, each one should retain the place in life that the Lord assigned to him and to which God has called him. This is the rule I lay down in all the churches.*n* 18Was a man already circumcised when he was called? He should not become uncircumcised. Was a man uncircumcised when he was called? He should not be circumcised.*o* 19Circumcision is nothing and uncircumcision is nothing.*p* Keeping God's commands is what counts. 20Each one should remain in the situation which he was in when God called him. 21Were you a slave when you were called? Don't let it trouble you—although if you can gain your freedom, do so. 22For he who was a slave when he was called by the Lord is the Lord's freedman;*q* similarly, he who was a free man when he was called is Christ's slave. 23You were bought at a price;*r* do not become slaves of men. 24Brothers, each man, as responsible to God, should remain in the situation God called him to.

25Now about virgins: I have no command from the Lord, but I give a judgment as one who by the Lord's mercy*s* is trustworthy. 26Because of the present crisis, I

7:14 *k*Mal 2:15
7:15 *l*Ro 14:19
7:16 *m*1Pe 3:1
7:17 *n*1Co 4:17
7:18 *o*Ac 15:1, 2
7:19 *p*Gal 5:6
7:22 *q*Jn 8:32, 36
7:23 *r*1Co 6:20
7:25 *s*1Ti 1:13, 16

7:12 Paul's *command* about the permanence of marriage (7:10) comes from the Old Testament (Genesis 2:24) and from Jesus (Mark 10:2–12). His *suggestion* in this verse is based on God's command, and Paul applies it to the situation the Corinthians were facing. Paul ranked the command above the suggestion because one is an eternal principle while the other is a specific application. Nevertheless, for people in similar situations, Paul's suggestion is the best advice they will get. Paul was a man of God, an apostle, and he had the mind of Christ.

●**7:12–14** Because of their desire to serve Christ, some people in the Corinthian church thought they ought to divorce their pagan spouses and marry Christians. But Paul affirmed the marriage commitment. God's ideal is for marriages to stay together—even when one spouse is not a believer. The Christian spouse should try to win the other to Christ. It would be easy to rationalize leaving; however, Paul makes a strong case for staying with the unbelieving spouse and being a positive influence on the marriage. Paul, like Jesus, believed that marriage is permanent (see Mark 10:1–9).

7:14 The blessings that flow to believers don't stop there, but extend to others. God regards the marriage as "sanctified" (set apart for his use) by the presence of one Christian spouse. The other does not receive salvation automatically, but is helped by this relationship. The children of such a marriage are to be regarded as "holy" (because of God's blessing on the family unit) until they are old enough to decide for themselves.

7:15, 16 This verse is misused by some as a loophole to get out of marriage. But Paul's statements were given to encourage the Christian spouse to try to get along with the unbeliever and make the marriage work. If, however, the unbelieving spouse insisted on leaving, Paul said to let him or her go. The only alternative would be for the Christian to deny his or her faith to preserve the marriage, and that would be worse than dissolving the marriage. Paul's chief purpose in writing this was to urge the married couples to seek unity, not separation (see 7:17; 1 Peter 3:1, 2).

7:17 Apparently the Corinthians were ready to make wholesale changes without thinking through the ramifications. Paul was writing to say that people should be Christians where they are. You can do God's work and demonstrate your faith *anywhere.* If you became a Christian after marriage, and your spouse is not a believer, remember that you don't have to be married to a Christian to live for Christ. Don't assume that you are in the wrong place, or stuck with the wrong person. You may be just where God wants you (see 7:20).

7:18, 19 The ceremony of circumcision was an important part of the Jews' relationship with God. In fact, before Christ came, circumcision was commanded by God for those who claimed to follow him (Genesis 17:9–14). But after Christ's death, circumcision was no longer necessary (Acts 15; Romans 4:9–11; Galatians 5:2–4; Colossians 2:11). Pleasing God and obeying him is more important than observing traditional ceremonies.

●**7:20** Often we are so concerned about what we *could* be doing for God somewhere else that we miss great opportunities right where we are. Paul says that when someone becomes a Christian, he or she should usually continue with the work he or she has previously been doing—provided it isn't immoral or unethical. Every job can become Christian work when you realize that the purpose of your life is to honor, serve, and speak out for Christ. Because God has placed you where you are, look carefully for opportunities to serve him there.

7:23 Slavery was common throughout the Roman empire. Some Christians in the Corinthian church were undoubtedly slaves. Paul said that although the Christian slaves were slaves to other human beings, they were free from the power of sin in their lives. People today are slaves to sin until they commit their lives to Christ, who alone can conquer sin's power. Sin, pride, and fear no longer have any claim over us, just as a slave owner no longer has power over the slaves he has sold. The Bible says we become Christ's slaves when we become Christians (Romans 6:18), but this actually

7:26
t ver 1, 8

think that it is good for you to remain as you are. *t* 27 Are you married? Do not seek a divorce. Are you unmarried? Do not look for a wife. 28 But if you do marry, you have not sinned; and if a virgin marries, she has not sinned. But those who marry will face many troubles in this life, and I want to spare you this.

7:29
u Ro 13:11, 12

29 What I mean, brothers, is that the time is short. *u* From now on those who have wives should live as if they had none; 30 those who mourn, as if they did not; those who are happy, as if they were not; those who buy something, as if it were not theirs to keep; 31 those who use the things of the world, as if not engrossed in them. For this world in its present form is passing away.

7:32
v 1 Ti 5:5

32 I would like you to be free from concern. An unmarried man is concerned about the Lord's affairs *v* — how he can please the Lord. 33 But a married man is concerned about the affairs of this world — how he can please his wife — 34 and his interests are divided. An unmarried woman or virgin is concerned about the Lord's affairs: Her aim is to be devoted to the Lord in both body and spirit. But a married woman is concerned about the affairs of this world — how she can please her husband. 35 I am saying this for your own good, not to restrict you, but that you may live in a right way in undivided devotion to the Lord.

36 If anyone thinks he is acting improperly toward the virgin he is engaged to, and if she is getting along in years and he feels he ought to marry, he should do as he wants. He is not sinning. They should get married. 37 But the man who has settled the matter in his own mind, who is under no compulsion but has control over his own will, and who has made up his mind not to marry the virgin — this man also does the right thing. 38 So then, he who marries the virgin does right, but he who does not marry her does even better. *q*

7:39
w Ro 7:2, 3
x 2 Co 6:14

39 A woman is bound to her husband as long as he lives. *w* But if her husband dies, she is free to marry anyone she wishes, but he must belong to the Lord. *x* 40 In my judgment, she is happier if she stays as she is — and I think that I too have the Spirit of God.

q 36-38 Or 36 If anyone thinks he is not treating his daughter properly, and if she is getting along in years, and he feels she ought to marry, he should do as he wants. He is not sinning. He should let her get married. 37 But the man who has settled the matter in his own mind, who is under no compulsion but has control over his own will, and who has made up his mind to keep the virgin unmarried — this man also does the right thing. 38 So then, he who gives his virgin in marriage does right, but he who does not give her in marriage does even better.

---

means we gain our freedom, because sin no longer controls us.

7:26 Paul probably foresaw the impending persecution that the Roman government would soon bring upon Christians. He gave this practical advice because being unmarried would mean less suffering and more freedom to throw one's life into the cause of Christ (7:29), even to the point of fearlessly dying for him. Paul's advice reveals his single-minded devotion to spreading the Good News.

● **7:28** Many people naively think that marriage will solve all their problems. Here are some problems marriage won't solve: (1) loneliness, (2) sexual temptation, (3) satisfaction of one's deepest emotional needs, (4) elimination of life's difficulties. Marriage alone does not hold two people together, but commitment does — commitment to Christ and to each other despite conflicts and problems. As wonderful as it is, marriage does not automatically solve every problem. Whether married or single, we must be content with our situation and focus on Christ, not on loved ones, to help address our problems.

7:29 Paul urges all believers to make the most of their time before Christ's return. Every person in every generation should have this sense of urgency about telling the Good News to others. Life is short — there's not much time!

7:29-31 Paul urges believers not to regard marriage, home, or financial security as the ultimate goals of life. As much as possible, we should live unhindered by the cares of this world, not getting involved with burdensome mortgages, budgets, investments, or

debts that might keep us from doing God's work. A married man or woman, as Paul points out (7:33, 34), must take care of earthly responsibilities — but they should make every effort to keep them modest and manageable.

7:32-34 Some single people feel tremendous pressure to be married. They think their lives can be complete only with a spouse. But Paul underlines one advantage of being single — the potential of a greater focus on Christ and his work. If you are unmarried, use your special opportunity to serve Christ wholeheartedly.

7:38 When Paul says the unmarried person does even better, he is talking about the potential time available for service to God. The single person does not have the responsibility of caring for a spouse and raising a family. Singleness, however, does not ensure service to God — involvement in service depends on the commitment of the individual.

7:40 Paul's advice comes from the Holy Spirit, who guides and equips both single and married people to fulfill their roles.

2. Instruction on Christian freedom
Food Sacrificed to Idols

8 Now about food sacrificed to idols:*y* We know that we all possess knowledge.*r* Knowledge puffs up, but love builds up. *2*The man who thinks he
knows something does not yet know as he ought to know.*z* *3*But the man who
loves God is known by God.*a*

*4*So then, about eating food sacrificed to idols: We know that an idol is nothing
at all in the world and that there is no God but one.*b* *5*For even if there are so-called
gods, whether in heaven or on earth (as indeed there are many "gods" and many
"lords"), *6*yet for us there is but one God, the Father,*c* from whom all things
came*d* and for whom we live; and there is but one Lord, Jesus Christ, through
whom all things came and through whom we live.

*7*But not everyone knows this. Some people are still so accustomed to idols that
when they eat such food they think of it as having been sacrificed to an idol, and
since their conscience is weak,*e* it is defiled. *8*But food does not bring us near to
God;*f* we are no worse if we do not eat, and no better if we do.

*9*Be careful, however, that the exercise of your freedom does not become a stumbling block*g* to the weak. *10*For if anyone with a weak conscience sees you who
have this knowledge eating in an idol's temple, won't he be emboldened to eat what
has been sacrificed to idols? *11*So this weak brother, for whom Christ died, is destroyed*h* by your knowledge. *12*When you sin against your brothers in this way and
wound their weak conscience, you sin against Christ. *13*Therefore, if what I eat
causes my brother to fall into sin, I will never eat meat again, so that I will not cause
him to fall.

The Rights of an Apostle

9 Am I not free? Am I not an apostle?*i* Have I not seen Jesus our Lord? Are you
not the result of my work in the Lord?*j* *2*Even though I may not be an apostle
to others, surely I am to you! For you are the seal of my apostleship in the Lord.

*3*This is my defense to those who sit in judgment on me. *4*Don't we have the right
to food and drink? *5*Don't we have the right to take a believing wife along with us,

r 1 *Or "We all possess knowledge," as you say*

8:1
y Ac 15:20

8:2
z 1Co 13:8, 9, 12;
1Ti 6:4

8:3
a Gal 4:9

8:4
b Dt 6:4

8:6
c Mal 2:10
d Ro 11:36

8:7
e Ro 14:14

8:8
f Ro 14:17

8:9
g Gal 5:13

8:11
h Ro 14:15, 20

9:1
i 2Co 12:12
j 1Co 3:6

● **8:1** Meat bought in the marketplace was likely to have been sym-
bolically offered to an idol in one of the many pagan temples. Animals were brought to a temple, killed before an idol as part of a
pagan religious ceremony, and eaten at a feast in the idol's temple
or taken to butchers who sold the meat in the marketplace. The believers wondered if by eating such meat, they were somehow participating in the worship of pagan idols.

8:1-3 Love is more important than knowledge. Knowledge can
make us look good and feel important, but we can all too easily develop an arrogant, know-it-all attitude. Many people with strong
opinions are unwilling to listen to and learn from God and others.
We can obtain God's knowledge only by loving him (see James
3:17, 18). And we can know and be known by God only when we
model him by showing love (1 John 4:7, 8).

● **8:4-9** Paul addressed these words to believers who weren't
bothered by eating meat that had been sacrificed to idols. Although idols were phony, and the pagan ritual of sacrificing to
them was meaningless, eating such meat offended Christians with
more sensitive consciences. Paul said, therefore, that if a weaker
or less mature believer misunderstood their actions, they should,
out of consideration, avoid eating meat offered to idols.

● **8:10-13** Christian freedom does not mean that anything goes. It
means that our salvation is not determined by good deeds or legalistic rules, but by the free gift of God (Ephesians 2:8, 9). Christian
freedom, then, is inseparably tied to Christian responsibility. New
believers are often very sensitive to what is right or wrong, what
they should or shouldn't do. Some actions may be perfectly all
right for us to do, but may harm a Christian brother or sister who is

still young in the faith and learning what the Christian life is all
about. We must be careful not to offend a sensitive or younger
Christian or, by our example, to cause him or her to sin. When we
love others, our freedom should be less important to us than
strengthening the faith of a brother or sister in Christ.

9:1 Some Corinthians were questioning Paul's authority and
rights as an apostle, so Paul gave his credentials – he actually saw
and talked with the resurrected Christ, who called him to be an
apostle (see Acts 9:3–18). Such credentials make the advice he
gives in this letter more persuasive. In 2 Corinthians 10 – 13, Paul
defends his apostleship in greater detail.

9:1 Changed lives were the evidence that God was using Paul.
Does your faith have an impact on others? You can be a life-
changer, helping others grow spiritually, if you dedicate yourself to
being used by God and letting him make you effective.

● **9:4ff** Paul uses himself as an illustration of giving up personal
rights. Paul had the right to hospitality, to be married, and to be
paid for his work. But he willingly gave up these rights to win people to Christ. When your focus is on living for Christ, your rights become comparatively unimportant.

9:4-10 Jesus said that workers deserve their wages (Luke 10:7).
Paul echoes this thought and urges the church to be sure to pay
their Christian workers. We have the responsibility to care for our
pastors, teachers, and other spiritual leaders. It is our duty to see
that those who serve us in the ministry are fairly and adequately
compensated.

9:5 The brothers of Jesus attained leadership status in the
church at Jerusalem. James (one of the "Lord's brothers"), for ex-

as do the other apostles and the Lord's brothers and Cephas[s]? 6Or is it only I and
Barnabas who must work for a living?
7Who serves as a soldier at his own expense? Who plants a vineyard[k] and does
not eat of its grapes? Who tends a flock and does not drink of the milk? 8Do I say
this merely from a human point of view? Doesn't the Law say the same thing? 9For
it is written in the Law of Moses: "Do not muzzle an ox while it is treading out the
grain."[t][l] Is it about oxen that God is concerned? 10Surely he says this for us,
doesn't he? Yes, this was written for us, because when the plowman plows and the
thresher threshes, they ought to do so in the hope of sharing in the harvest. 11If we
have sown spiritual seed among you, is it too much if we reap a material harvest
from you?[m] 12If others have this right of support from you, shouldn't we have it all
the more?
But we did not use this right. On the contrary, we put up with anything rather
than hinder[n] the gospel of Christ. 13Don't you know that those who work in the
temple get their food from the temple, and those who serve at the altar share in what
is offered on the altar?[o] 14In the same way, the Lord has commanded that those
who preach the gospel should receive their living from the gospel.
15But I have not used any of these rights.[p] And I am not writing this in the hope
that you will do such things for me. I would rather die than have anyone deprive me
of this boast.[q] 16Yet when I preach the gospel, I cannot boast, for I am compelled
to preach.[r] Woe to me if I do not preach the gospel! 17If I preach voluntarily, I
have a reward;[s] if not voluntarily, I am simply discharging the trust committed to
me.[t] 18What then is my reward? Just this: that in preaching the gospel I may offer
it free of charge, and so not make use of my rights in preaching it.
19Though I am free and belong to no man, I make myself a slave to everyone,[u]
to win as many as possible.[v] 20To the Jews I became like a Jew, to win the Jews.[w]
To those under the law I became like one under the law (though I myself am not
under the law), so as to win those under the law. 21To those not having the law I

[s] 5 That is, Peter [t] 9 Deut. 25:4

9:7 [k] Dt 20:6
9:9 [l] Dt 25:4; 1Ti 5:18
9:11 [m] Ro 15:27
9:12 [n] 2Co 11:7-12
9:13 [o] Lev 6:16, 26
9:15 [p] Ac 18:3 [q] 2Co 11:9, 10
9:16 [r] Ro 1:14
9:17 [s] 1Co 3:8, 14 [t] Gal 2:7; Col 1:25
9:19 [u] Gal 5:13 [v] Mt 18:15
9:20 [w] Ac 16:3

STRONGER, WEAKER BELIEVERS

Advice to:	
Stronger believer	Don't be proud of your maturity; don't flaunt your freedom. Act in love so you do not cause a weaker believer to stumble.
Weaker believer	Although you may not feel the same freedom in some areas as in others, take your time, pray to God, but do not force others to adhere to your stipulations. You would hinder other believers by making up rules and standards for how everyone ought to behave. Make sure your convictions are based on God's Word, and are not simply an expression of your opinions.
Pastors and leaders	Teach correctly from God's Word, helping Christians understand what is right and wrong in God's eyes, and helping them see that they can have varied opinions on other issues and still be unified. Don't allow potential problems to get out of hand, causing splits and divisions.

Paul advises those who are more mature in the faith about how they must care about their brothers and sisters in Christ who have more tender consciences; those "weaker" brothers and sisters are advised concerning their growth; and pastors and leaders are instructed on how to deal with the conflicts that easily could arise between these groups.

ample, led the way to an agreement at the Jerusalem council in Acts 15, and wrote the book of James.

9:13 As part of their pay, priests in the temple would receive a portion of the offerings as their food (see Numbers 18:8–24).

9:16 Preaching the gospel was Paul's gift and calling, and he said he couldn't stop preaching even if he wanted to. Paul was driven by the desire to do what God wanted, using his gifts for God's glory. What special gifts has God given you? Are you motivated, like Paul, to honor God with your gifts?

9:19–27 In 9:19–22 Paul asserts that he has freedom to do anything; in 9:24–27 he emphasizes a life of strict discipline. The Christian life involves both freedom and discipline. The goals of Paul's life were to glorify God and bring people to Christ. Thus he stayed free of any philosophical position or material entanglement that might sidetrack him, while he strictly disciplined himself to carry out his goal. For Paul, both freedom and discipline were important tools to be used in God's service.

became like one not having the law^x (though I am not free from God's law but am
under Christ's law), so as to win those not having the law. ²²To the weak I became
weak, to win the weak. I have become all things to all men so that by all possible
means I might save some. ²³I do all this for the sake of the gospel, that I may share
in its blessings.

·²⁴Do you not know that in a race all the runners run, but only one gets the prize?
Run^y in such à way as to get the prize. ²⁵Everyone who competes in the games
goes into strict training. They do it to get a crown that will not last; but we do it to
get a crown that will last forever. ²⁶Therefore I do not run like a man running aim-
lessly; I do not fight like a man beating the air. ²⁷No, I beat my body^z and make
it my slave so that after I have preached to others, I myself will not be disqualified
for the prize.

Warnings From Israel's History

10 For I do not want you to be ignorant of the fact, brothers, that our forefathers
were all under the cloud^a and that they all passed through the sea.^b ²They
were all baptized into Moses in the cloud and in the sea. ³They all ate the same
spiritual food ⁴and drank the same spiritual drink; for they drank from the spiritual
rock^c that accompanied them, and that rock was Christ. ⁵Nevertheless, God was
not pleased with most of them; their bodies were scattered over the desert.^d

⁶Now these things occurred as examples^u to keep us from setting our hearts on
evil things as they did. ⁷Do not be idolaters, as some of them were; as it is written:
"The people sat down to eat and drink and got up to indulge in pagan revelry."^v
⁸We should not commit sexual immorality, as some of them did—and in one day
twenty-three thousand of them died. ⁹We should not test the Lord, as some of them
did—and were killed by snakes.^e ¹⁰And do not grumble, as some of them
did—and were killed by the destroying angel.^f

¹¹These things happened to them as examples and were written down as warn-
ings for us, on whom the fulfillment of the ages has come. ¹²So, if you think you
are standing firm,^g be careful that you don't fall! ¹³No temptation has seized you
^u 6 Or *types*; also in verse 11   ^v 7 Exodus 32:6

9:21
^xRo 2:12, 14

9:24
^y2Ti 4:7

9:27
^zRo 8:13

10:1
^aEx 13:21
^bEx 14:22, 29

10:4
^cEx 17:6

10:5
^dNu 14:29

10:9
^eNu 21:5, 6

10:10
^fEx 12:23

10:12
^gRo 11:20

9:22, 23 Paul gives several important principles for ministry:
(1) find common ground with those you contact; (2) avoid a know-
it-all attitude; (3) make others feel accepted; (4) be sensitive to
their needs and concerns; and (5) look for opportunities to tell
them about Christ. These principles are just as valid for us as they
were for Paul.

● **9:24-27** Winning a race requires purpose and discipline. Paul
uses this illustration to explain that the Christian life takes hard
work, self-denial, and grueling preparation. As Christians, we are
running toward our heavenly reward. The essential disciplines of
prayer, Bible study, and worship equip us to run with vigor and
stamina. Don't merely observe from the grandstand; don't just turn
out to jog a couple of laps each morning. Train diligently—your
spiritual progress depends upon it.

9:25 At times we must even give up something good in order to
do what God wants. Each person's special duties determine the
discipline and denial that he or she must accept. Without a goal,
discipline is nothing but self-punishment. With the goal of pleasing
God, our denial seems like nothing compared to the eternal, imperishable reward that will be ours.

● **9:27** When Paul says he might be disqualified, he does not mean
that he could lose his salvation, but rather that he could lose his
privilege of telling others about Christ. It is easy to tell others how
to live and then not to take our own advice. We must be careful to
practice what we preach.

10:1ff In chapter 9 Paul used himself as an example of a mature
Christian who disciplines himself to better serve God. In chapter
10, he uses Israel as an example of spiritual immaturity, shown in
their overconfidence and lack of self-discipline.

● **10:1-5** The cloud and the sea mentioned here refer to Israel's
escape from slavery in Egypt when God led them by a cloud and
brought them safely through the Red Sea (Exodus 14). The spiritual food and drink are the miraculous provisions God gave as they
traveled through the desert (Exodus 15; 16).

10:2 "Baptized into Moses" means that just as we are united in
Christ by baptism, so the Israelites were united under Moses' leadership in the events of the exodus.

● **10:7-10** The incident referred to in 10:7 is when the Israelites
made a golden calf and worshiped it in the desert (Exodus 32).
The incident in 10:8 is recorded in Numbers 25:1-9 when the Israelites worshiped Baal of Peor and engaged in sexual immorality
with Moabite women. The reference in 10:9 is to the Israelites'
complaint about their food (Numbers 21:5, 6). They put the Lord to
the test by seeing how far they could go. In 10:10, Paul refers to
when the people complained against Moses and Aaron, and the
plague that resulted (Numbers 14:2, 36; 16:41-50). The destroying
angel is referred to in Exodus 12:23.

● **10:11** Today's pressures make it easy to ignore or forget the lessons of the past. But Paul cautions us to remember the lessons the
Israelites learned about God so we can avoid repeating their errors. The key to remembering is to study the Bible regularly so that
these lessons remind us of how God wants us to live. We need not
repeat their mistakes!

10:13 In a culture filled with moral depravity and sin-inducing
pressures, Paul gave strong encouragement to the Corinthians
about temptation. He said: (1) wrong desires and temptations happen to everyone, so don't feel you've been singled out; (2) others
have resisted temptation, and so can you; (3) any temptation can
be resisted because God will help you resist it. God helps you re-

10:13
h 2Pe 2:9

except what is common to man. And God is faithful; he will not let you be tempted beyond what you can bear. h But when you are tempted, he will also provide a way out so that you can stand up under it.

Idol Feasts and the Lord's Supper

14Therefore, my dear friends, flee from idolatry. 15I speak to sensible people; judge for yourselves what I say. 16Is not the cup of thanksgiving for which we give thanks a participation in the blood of Christ? And is not the bread that we break a

10:16
i Mt 26:26-28

participation in the body of Christ? i 17Because there is one loaf, we, who are many, are one body, for we all partake of the one loaf.

18Consider the people of Israel: Do not those who eat the sacrifices participate in the altar? 19Do I mean then that a sacrifice offered to an idol is anything, or that an idol is anything? 20No, but the sacrifices of pagans are offered to demons, j not to God, and I do not want you to be participants with demons. 21You cannot drink the

10:20
j Dt 32:17;
Ps 106:37
10:21
k 2Co 6:15, 16
10:22
l Dt 32:16, 21

cup of the Lord and the cup of demons too; you cannot have a part in both the Lord's table and the table of demons. k 22Are we trying to arouse the Lord's jealousy? l Are we stronger than he?

WHY WE DON'T GIVE UP	Reference	The Purpose	The Plan	The Prize
Perseverance, persistence, the prize!! The Christian life was never promised as an easy way to live; instead, Paul constantly reminds us that we must have a purpose and a plan because times will be difficult and Satan will attack. But we never persevere without the promise of a prize—a promise God will keep.	1 Corinthians 9:24–27	● Run to get the prize ● Run straight to the goal	● Deny yourself whatever is potentially harmful ● Discipline your body, training it	● A crown that will last forever
	Galatians 6:7–10	● Don't become weary in doing good ● Don't get discouraged and give up ● Do good to everyone	● Sow to please the Spirit	● Reap eternal life
	Ephesians 6:10–20	● Put on the full armor of God ● Pray on all occasions	● Use all the pieces of God's armor provided for you	● Taking our stand against the devil's schemes
	Philippians 3:12–14	● Press on toward the day when you will be all God wants you to be	● Forget the past, strain toward what is ahead	● The prize for which God calls us heavenward
	2 Timothy 2:1–13	● Entrust these great truths to people who will teach them to others ● Be strong in Christ's grace, even when your faith is faltering	● Endure hardship like a soldier, and don't get involved in worldly affairs ● Follow the Lord's rules, as an athlete must do in order to win ● Work hard, like a farmer who tends his crops for the harvest	● We will live with Christ; we will reign with him ● He always remains faithful to us and always carries out his promises

sist temptation by helping you (1) recognize those people and situations that give you trouble, (2) run from anything you know is wrong, (3) choose to do only what is right, (4) pray for God's help, and (5) seek friends who love God and can offer help when you are tempted. Running from a tempting situation is your first step on the way to victory (see 2 Timothy 2:22).

10:14 Idol worship was the major expression of religion in Corinth. There were several pagan temples in the city, and they were very popular. The statues of wood or stone were not evil in themselves, but people gave them credit for what only God could do, such as provide good weather, crops, and children. Idolatry is still a serious problem today, but it takes a different form. We don't put our trust in statues of wood and stone, but in paper money and plastic cards. Trusting anything for what God alone provides is idolatry. Our modern idols are those symbols of power, pleasure, or prestige that we so highly regard. When we understand contemporary parallels to idolatry, Paul's words to "flee from idolatry" become much more meaningful.

●**10:16–21** The idea of unity and fellowship with God through eating a sacrifice was strong in Judaism and Christianity as well as in paganism. In Old Testament days, when a Jew offered a sacrifice, he ate a part of that sacrifice as a way of restoring his unity with God, against whom he had sinned (Deuteronomy 12:17, 18). Similarly, Christians participate in Christ's once-for-all sacrifice when they eat the bread and drink the wine symbolizing his body and blood. Recent converts from paganism could not help being affected if they knowingly ate with pagans in their feasts the meat offered to idols.

●**10:21** As followers of Christ we must give him our total allegiance. We cannot, as Paul explains, have a part in "both the Lord's table and the table of demons." Eating at the Lord's table means communing with Christ and identifying with his death. Eating at the demons' table means identifying with Satan by worshiping or promoting pagan (or evil) activities. Are you trying to lead two lives, following the desires of both Christ and the crowd? The Bible says that you can't do both at the same time.

The Believer's Freedom

23"Everything is permissible" — but not everything is beneficial.*m* "Everything is permissible" — but not everything is constructive. 24Nobody should seek his own good, but the good of others. *n*

25Eat anything sold in the meat market without raising questions of conscience, 26for, "The earth is the Lord's, and everything in it."*w o*

27If some unbeliever invites you to a meal and you want to go, eat whatever is put before you*p* without raising questions of conscience. 28But if anyone says to you, "This has been offered in sacrifice," then do not eat it, both for the sake of the man who told you and for conscience' sake*x* — 29the other man's conscience, I mean, not yours. For why should my freedom be judged by another's conscience? 30If I take part in the meal with thankfulness, why am I denounced because of something I thank God for?*q*

31So whether you eat or drink or whatever you do, do it all for the glory of God.*r* 32Do not cause anyone to stumble, whether Jews, Greeks or the church of God*s* — 33even as I try to please everybody in every way.*t* For I am not seeking my own

11 good but the good of many, so that they may be saved. 1Follow my example, as I follow the example of Christ.

3. Instruction on public worship

Propriety in Worship

2I praise you for remembering me in everything*u* and for holding to the teachings,*y* just as I passed them on to you.

w 26 Psalm 24:1   *x 28* Some manuscripts *conscience' sake, for "the earth is the Lord's and everything in it"*
y 2 Or *traditions*

10:23
m 1Co 6:12

10:24
n Ro 15:1, 2

10:26
o Ps 24:1

10:27
p Lk 10:7

10:30
q Ro 14:6

10:31
r Col 3:17;
1Pe 4:11

10:32
s Ac 20:28

10:33
t Ro 15:2

11:2
u 1Co 4:17

●**10:23, 24** Sometimes it's hard to know when to defer to the weaker believer. Paul gives a simple rule of thumb to help in making the decision — we should be sensitive and gracious. While some actions may not be wrong, they may not be in the best interest of others. While we have freedom in Christ, we shouldn't exercise our freedom at the cost of hurting a Christian brother or sister. We are not to consider only ourselves, but we must be sensitive to others. For more on the proper attitude toward a weaker believer, see the notes on 8:10–13 and Romans 14.

10:25–27 Paul gave one answer to the dilemma — to buy whatever meat is sold at the market without asking whether it was offered to idols. It doesn't matter anyway, and no one's conscience would be troubled. When we become too worried about our every action, we become legalistic and cannot enjoy life. Everything belongs to God, and he has given us all things to enjoy. If we know something is a problem, then we can deal with it, but we don't need to go looking for problems.

●**10:28–33** Why should we be limited by another person's conscience? Simply because we are to do all things for God's glory, even our eating and drinking. Nothing we do should cause another believer to stumble. We do what is best for others, so that they might be saved. On the other hand, Christians should not make a career out of being the weaker person with oversensitive consciences. Christian leaders and teachers should carefully teach about the freedom we have in matters not expressly forbidden by Scripture.

●**10:31** God's love must so permeate our motives that all we do will be for his glory. Keep this as a guiding principle by asking, "Is this action glorifying God?" or "How can I honor God through this action?"

10:33 Paul's criterion for all his actions was not what he liked best, but what was best for those around him. The opposite attitude would be: (1) being insensitive and doing what we want, no matter who is hurt by it; (2) being oversensitive and doing nothing, for fear that someone may be displeased; (3) being a "yes person" by going along with everything, trying to gain approval from people rather than from God. In this age of "me first" and "looking out for

number one," Paul's startling statement is a good standard. If we make the good of others one of our primary goals, we will develop a serving attitude that pleases God.

11:1 Why did Paul say, "Follow my example"? Paul wasn't being arrogant — he did not think of himself as sinless. At this time, however, the Corinthian believers did not know much about the life and ministry of Christ. Paul could not tell them to imitate Jesus, because the Gospels had not yet been written, so they did not know what Jesus was like. The best way to point these new Christians to Christ was to point them to a Christian whom they trusted (see also Galatians 4:12; Philippians 3:17; 1 Thessalonians 1:6; 2:14; 2 Thessalonians 3:7, 9). Paul had been in Corinth almost two years and had built a relationship of trust with many of these new believers.

11:2ff In this section Paul's main concern is irreverence in worship. We need to read it in the context of the situation in Corinth. The matter of wearing hats or head coverings, although seemingly insignificant, had become a big problem because two cultural backgrounds were colliding. Jewish women always covered their heads in worship. For a woman to uncover her head in public was a sign of loose morals. On the other hand, Greek women may have been used to worshiping without head coverings.

In this letter Paul had already spoken about divisions and disorder in the church. Both are involved in this issue. Paul's solution comes from his desire for unity among church members and for appropriateness in the worship service. He accepted God's sovereignty in creating the rules for relationships.

●**11:2–16** This section focuses primarily on proper attitudes and conduct in worship, not on the marriage relationship or on the role of women in the church. While Paul's specific instructions may be cultural (women covering their heads in worship), the principles behind his specific instructions are timeless, principles like respect for spouse, reverence and appropriateness in worship, and focus of all of life on God. If anything you do can easily offend members and divide the church, then change your ways to promote church unity. Thus Paul told the women who were not wearing head coverings to wear them, not because it was a Scriptural command, but because it kept the congregation from dividing over a petty issue that served only to take people's minds off Christ.

11:3
vEph 5:23

11:5
wAc 21:9
xDt 21:12

11:7
yGe 1:26

11:8
zGe 2:21-23

11:9
aGe 2:18

3Now I want you to realize that the head of every man is Christ, and the head of the woman is man,v and the head of Christ is God. 4Every man who prays or prophesies with his head covered dishonors his head. 5And every woman who prays or prophesiesw with her head uncovered dishonors her head — it is just as though her head were shaved.x 6If a woman does not cover her head, she should have her hair cut off; and if it is a disgrace for a woman to have her hair cut or shaved off, she should cover her head. 7A man ought not to cover his head,z since he is the imagey and glory of God; but the woman is the glory of man. 8For man did not come from woman, but woman from man;z 9neither was man created for woman, but woman for man.a 10For this reason, and because of the angels, the woman ought to have a sign of authority on her head.

11In the Lord, however, woman is not independent of man, nor is man independent of woman. 12For as woman came from man, so also man is born of woman. But everything comes from God. 13Judge for yourselves: Is it proper for a woman to pray to God with her head uncovered? 14Does not the very nature of things teach

z 4-7 Or 4Every man who prays or prophesies with long hair dishonors his head. 5And every woman who prays or prophesies with no covering ,of hair, on her head dishonors her head—she is just like one of the "shorn women." 6If a woman has no covering, let her be for now with short hair, but since it is a disgrace for a woman to have her hair shorn or shaved, she should grow it again. 7A man ought not to have long hair

MAKING CHOICES IN SENSITIVE ISSUES

If I choose one course of action:

. . . does it help my witness for Christ? (9:19–22)

. . . am I motivated by a desire to help others to know Christ? (9:23; 10:33)

. . . does it help me do my best? (9:25)

. . . is it against a specific command in Scripture and would thus cause me to sin? (10:12)

. . . is it the best and most beneficial course of action? (10:23, 33)

. . . am I thinking only of myself, or do I truly care about the other person? (10:24)

. . . am I acting lovingly or selfishly? (10:28–31)

. . . does it glorify God? (10:31)

. . . will it cause someone else to sin? (10:32)

All of us make hundreds of choices every day. Most choices have no right or wrong attached to them—like what you wear or what you eat. But we always face decisions that carry a little more weight. We don't want to do wrong, and we don't want to cause others to do wrong, so how can we make such decisions?

●**11:3** In the phrase, "the head of the woman is man," *head* is not used to indicate control or supremacy, but rather, "the source of." Because man was created first, the woman derives her existence from man, as man does from Christ and Christ from God. Evidently Paul was correcting some excesses in worship that the emancipated Corinthian women were engaging in.

11:3 Submission is a key element in the smooth functioning of any business, government, or family. God ordained submission in certain relationships to prevent chaos. It is essential to understand that submission is not surrender, withdrawal, or apathy. It does not mean inferiority, because God created all people in his image and because all have equal value. Submission is mutual commitment and cooperation.

Thus God calls for submission among *equals*. He did not make the man superior; he made a way for the man and woman to work together. Jesus Christ, although equal with God the Father, submitted to him to carry out the plan for salvation. Likewise, although equal to man under God, the wife should submit to her husband for the sake of their marriage and family. Submission between equals is submission by choice, not by force. We serve God in these relationships by willingly submitting to others in our church, to our spouses, and to our government leaders.

●**11:9–11** God created lines of authority in order for his created world to function smoothly. Although there must be lines of authority, even in marriage, there should *not* be lines of superiority. God

created men and women with unique and complementary characteristics. One sex is not better than the other. We must not let the issue of authority and submission become a wedge to destroy oneness in marriage. Instead, we should use our unique gifts to strengthen our marriages and to glorify God.

11:10 "Because of the angels, the woman ought to have a sign of authority on her head" may mean that the woman should wear a covering on her head as a sign that she is under the man's authority. This is a fact even the angels understand as they observe Christians in worship. See the note on 11:2ff for an explanation of head coverings.

●**11:14, 15** In talking about head coverings and length of hair, Paul is saying that believers should look and behave in ways that are honorable within their own culture. In many cultures long hair on men is considered appropriate and masculine. In Corinth, it was thought to be a sign of male prostitution in the pagan temples. And women with short hair were labeled prostitutes. Paul was saying that in the Corinthian culture, Christian women should keep their hair long. If short hair on women was a sign of prostitution, then a Christian woman with short hair would find it even more difficult to be a believable witness for Jesus Christ. Paul wasn't saying we should adopt all the practices of our culture, but that we should avoid appearances and behavior that detract from our ultimate goal of being believable witnesses for Jesus Christ while demonstrating our Christian faith.

you that if a man has long hair, it is a disgrace to him, [15]but that if a woman has long hair, it is her glory? For long hair is given to her as a covering. [16]If anyone wants to be contentious about this, we have no other practice — nor do the churches of God. *b*

11:16
b 1Co 7:17

The Lord's Supper

[17]In the following directives I have no praise for you, *c* for your meetings do more harm than good. [18]In the first place, I hear that when you come together as a church, there are divisions *d* among you, and to some extent I believe it. [19]No doubt there have to be differences among you to show which of you have God's approval. *e* [20]When you come together, it is not the Lord's Supper you eat, [21]for as you eat, each of you goes ahead without waiting for anybody else. *f* One remains hungry, another gets drunk. [22]Don't you have homes to eat and drink in? Or do you despise the church of God *g* and humiliate those who have nothing? *h* What shall I say to you? Shall I praise you for this? Certainly not!

11:17
c ver 2, 22
11:18
d 1Co 1:10-12
11:19
e 1Jn 2:19
11:21
f Jude 12
11:22
g 1Co 10:32
h Jas 2:6

[23]For I received from the Lord what I also passed on to you: The Lord Jesus, on the night he was betrayed, took bread, [24]and when he had given thanks, he broke it and said, "This is my body, which is for you; do this in remembrance of me." [25]In the same way, after supper he took the cup, saying, "This cup is the new covenant *i* in my blood; do this, whenever you drink it, in remembrance of me." [26]For whenever you eat this bread and drink this cup, you proclaim the Lord's death until he comes.

11:25
i Lk 22:20

[27]Therefore, whoever eats the bread or drinks the cup of the Lord in an unworthy manner will be guilty of sinning against the body and blood of the Lord. [28]A man ought to examine himself *j* before he eats of the bread and drinks of the cup. [29]For

11:28
j 2Co 13:5

11:17-34 The Lord's Supper (11:20) is a visible representation of the Good News of the death of Christ for our sins. It reminds us of Christ's death and the glorious hope of his return. Our participation in it strengthens our faith through fellowship with Christ and with other believers.

11:19 Paul allows that there might be differences among church members. When they develop into self-willed divisions, they are destructive to the congregation. Those who cause division only serve to highlight those who are genuine believers.

●**11:21, 22** When the Lord's Supper was celebrated in the early church, it included a feast or fellowship meal followed by the celebration of Communion. In the church in Corinth, the fellowship meal had become a time when some ate and drank excessively while others went hungry. There was little sharing and caring. This certainly did not demonstrate the unity and love that should characterize the church, nor was it a preparation for Communion. Paul condemned these actions and reminded the church of the real purpose of the Lord's Supper.

11:24, 25 What does the Lord's Supper mean? The early church remembered that Jesus instituted the Lord's Supper on the night of the Passover meal (Luke 22:13-20). Just as Passover celebrated deliverance from slavery in Egypt, so the Lord's Supper celebrates deliverance from sin by Christ's death.

Christians pose several different possibilities for what Christ meant when he said, "This is my body." (1) Some believe that the wine and bread actually become Christ's physical blood and body. (2) Others believe that the bread and wine remain unchanged, but Christ is spiritually present with the bread and wine. (3) Still others believe that the bread and wine symbolize Christ's body and blood. Christians generally agree, however, that participating in the Lord's Supper is an important element in the Christian faith and that Christ's presence, however we understand it, strengthens us spiritually.

11:25 What is this new covenant? In the old covenant, people could approach God only through the priests and the sacrificial system. Jesus' death on the cross ushered in the new covenant or agreement between God and us. Now all people can personally approach God and communicate with him. The people of Israel first entered into this agreement after their exodus from Egypt (Exodus 24), and it was designed to point to the day when Jesus Christ would come. The new covenant completes, rather than replaces, the old covenant, fulfilling everything the old covenant looked forward to (see Jeremiah 31:31-34). Eating the bread and drinking the cup shows that we are remembering Christ's death for us and renewing our commitment to serve him.

11:25 Jesus said, "Do this, whenever you drink it, in remembrance of me." How do we remember Christ in the Lord's Supper? By thinking about what he did and why he did it. If the Lord's Supper becomes just a ritual or a pious habit, it no longer remembers Christ, and it loses its significance.

●**11:27ff** Paul gives specific instructions on how the Lord's Supper should be observed. (1) We should take the Lord's Supper thoughtfully because we are proclaiming that Christ died for our sins (11:26). (2) We should take it worthily, with due reverence and respect (11:27). (3) We should examine ourselves for any unconfessed sin or resentful attitude (11:28). We are to be properly prepared, based on our belief in and love for Christ. (4) We should be considerate of others (11:33), waiting until everyone is there and then eating in an orderly and unified manner.

●**11:27-34** When Paul said that no one should take the Lord's Supper in an unworthy manner, he was speaking to the church members who were rushing into it without thinking of its meaning. Those who did so were "guilty of sinning against the body and blood of the Lord." Instead of honoring his sacrifice, they were sharing in the guilt of those who crucified Christ. In reality, *no one* is worthy to take the Lord's Supper. We are all sinners saved by grace. This is why we should prepare ourselves for Communion through healthy introspection, confession of sin, and resolution of

anyone who eats and drinks without recognizing the body of the Lord eats and drinks judgment on himself. [30]That is why many among you are weak and sick, and a number of you have fallen asleep. [31]But if we judged ourselves, we would not come under judgment. [32]When we are judged by the Lord, we are being disciplined[k] so that we will not be condemned with the world.

[33]So then, my brothers, when you come together to eat, wait for each other. [34]If anyone is hungry, he should eat at home, so that when you meet together it may not result in judgment.

And when I come[l] I will give further directions.

Spiritual Gifts

12 Now about spiritual gifts,[m] brothers, I do not want you to be ignorant. [2]You know that when you were pagans, somehow or other you were influenced and led astray to mute idols.[n] [3]Therefore I tell you that no one who is speaking by the Spirit of God says, "Jesus be cursed," and no one can say, "Jesus is Lord," except by the Holy Spirit.[o]

[4]There are different kinds of gifts, but the same Spirit.[p] [5]There are different kinds of service, but the same Lord. [6]There are different kinds of working, but the same God works all of them in all men.

[7]Now to each one the manifestation of the Spirit is given for the common good. [8]To one there is given through the Spirit the message of wisdom,[q] to another the message of knowledge[r] by means of the same Spirit, [9]to another faith by the same Spirit, to another gifts of healing by that one Spirit, [10]to another miraculous powers,[s] to another prophecy, to another distinguishing between spirits,[t] to another speaking in different kinds of tongues,[a] and to still another the interpretation of tongues.[a] [11]All these are the work of one and the same Spirit, and he gives them to each one, just as he determines.

[a] 10 Or *languages*; also in verse 28

11:32
[k]Ps 94:12

11:34
[l]1Co 4:19

12:1
[m]Ro 1:11;
1Co 14:1, 37

12:2
[n]Ps 115:5

12:3
[o]1Jn 4:2, 3

12:4
[p]Ro 12:4-8

12:8
[q]1Co 2:6
[r]2Co 8:7

12:10
[s]Gal 3:5
[t]1Jn 4:1

---

differences with others. These actions remove the barriers that affect our relationship with Christ and with other believers. Awareness of your sin should not keep you away from Communion but should drive you to participate in it.

11:29 "Without recognizing the body of the Lord" means not understanding what the Lord's Supper means and not distinguishing it from a normal meal. Those who do so condemn themselves (see 11:27).

11:30 "Fallen asleep" is another way of describing death. That some of the people had died may have been a special supernatural judgment on the Corinthian church. This type of disciplinary judgment highlights the seriousness of the Communion service. The Lord's Supper is not to be taken lightly; this new covenant cost Jesus his life. It is not a meaningless ritual, but a sacrament given by Christ to help strengthen our faith.

11:34 People should come to this meal desiring to fellowship with other believers and prepare for the Lord's Supper to follow, not to fill up on a big dinner. "If anyone is hungry, he should eat at home" means that they should eat dinner beforehand, so as to come to the fellowship meal in the right frame of mind.

12:1ff The spiritual gifts given to each person by the Holy Spirit are special abilities that are to be used to minister to the needs of the body of believers. This chapter is not an exhaustive list of spiritual gifts (see Romans 12; Ephesians 4; 1 Peter 4:10, 11 for more examples). There are many gifts, people have different gifts, some people have more than one gift, and one gift is not superior to another. All spiritual gifts come from the Holy Spirit, and their purpose is to build up Christ's body, the church.

12:1ff Instead of building up and unifying the Corinthian church, the issue of spiritual gifts was splitting it. Spiritual gifts had become

symbols of spiritual power, causing rivalries because some people thought they were more "spiritual" than others because of their gifts. This was a terrible misuse of spiritual gifts because their purpose is always to help the church function more effectively, not to divide it. We can be divisive if we insist on using our gift our own way without being sensitive to others. We must never use gifts as a means of manipulating others or serving our own self-interest.

12:3 Anyone can claim to speak for God, and the world is full of false teachers. Paul gives us a test to help us discern whether or not a messenger is really from God: does he or she confess Christ as Lord? Don't naively accept the words of all who claim to speak for God; test their credentials by finding out what they teach about Christ.

12:9 All Christians have faith. Some, however, have the spiritual gift of faith, which is an unusual measure of trust in the Holy Spirit's power.

12:10, 11 "Prophecy" is not just a prediction about the future; it can also mean preaching God's Word with power. "Distinguishing between spirits" means the ability to discern whether a person who claims to speak for God is actually doing so, or is speaking by an evil spirit. (Paul discusses tongues and their interpretation in more detail in chapter 14.) No matter what gift(s) a person has, each gift is given by the Holy Spirit. The Holy Spirit decides which gifts each one of us should have. We are responsible to use and sharpen our gifts, but we can take no credit for what God has freely given us.

One Body, Many Parts

12The body is a unit, though it is made up of many parts; and though all its parts are many, they form one body. So it is with Christ. 13For we were all baptized by[b] one Spirit into one body — whether Jews or Greeks, slave or free[u] — and we were all given the one Spirit to drink.

14Now the body is not made up of one part but of many. 15If the foot should say, "Because I am not a hand, I do not belong to the body," it would not for that reason cease to be part of the body. 16And if the ear should say, "Because I am not an eye, I do not belong to the body," it would not for that reason cease to be part of the body. 17If the whole body were an eye, where would the sense of hearing be? If the whole body were an ear, where would the sense of smell be? 18But in fact God has arranged[v] the parts in the body, every one of them, just as he wanted them to be. 19If they were all one part, where would the body be? 20As it is, there are many parts, but one body.

21The eye cannot say to the hand, "I don't need you!" And the head cannot say to the feet, "I don't need you!" 22On the contrary, those parts of the body that seem to be weaker are indispensable, 23and the parts that we think are less honorable we treat with special honor. And the parts that are unpresentable are treated with special modesty, 24while our presentable parts need no special treatment. But God has combined the members of the body and has given greater honor to the parts that lacked it, 25so that there should be no division in the body, but that its parts should have equal concern for each other. 26If one part suffers, every part suffers with it; if one part is honored, every part rejoices with it.

27Now you are the body of Christ,[w] and each one of you is a part of it.[x] 28And in the church God has appointed first of all apostles,[y] second prophets, third teachers, then workers of miracles, also those having gifts of healing,[z] those able to help others, those with gifts of administration,[a] and those speaking in different kinds of tongues.[b] 29Are all apostles? Are all prophets? Are all teachers? Do all work miracles? 30Do all have gifts of healing? Do all speak in tongues[c]? Do all interpret? 31But eagerly desire[d] the greater gifts.

b 13 Or with; or in   c 30 Or other languages   d 31 Or But you are eagerly desiring

12:13 uGal 3:28; Col 3:11
12:18 vver 28
12:27 wEph 1:23; 4:12; Col 1:18, 24   xRo 12:5
12:28 yEph 4:11   zver 9   aRo 12:6-8   bver 10
12:31 c1Co 14:1, 39

●**12:12** Paul compares the body of Christ to a human body. Each part has a specific function that is necessary to the body as a whole. The parts are different for a purpose, and in their differences they must work together. Christians must avoid two common errors: (1) being too proud of their abilities, or (2) thinking they have nothing to give to the body of believers. Instead of comparing ourselves to one another, we should use our different gifts, together, to spread the Good News of salvation.

●**12:13** The church is composed of many types of people from a variety of backgrounds with a multitude of gifts and abilities. It is easy for these differences to divide people, as was the case in Corinth. But despite the differences, all believers have one thing in common — faith in Christ. On this essential truth the church finds unity. All believers are baptized by one Holy Spirit into one body of believers, the church. We don't lose our individual identities, but we have an overriding oneness in Christ. When a person becomes a Christian, the Holy Spirit takes up residence, and he or she is born into God's family. "We were all given the one Spirit to drink" means that the same Holy Spirit completely fills our innermost beings. As members of God's family, we may have different interests and gifts, but we have a common goal.

●**12:14-24** Using the analogy of the body, Paul emphasizes the importance of each church member (see the note on 12:12). If a seemingly insignificant part is taken away, the whole body becomes less effective. Thinking that your gift is more important than someone else's is an expression of spiritual pride. We should not look down on those who seem unimportant, and we should not be jealous of others who have impressive gifts. Instead, we should use the gifts we have been given and encourage others to use theirs. If we don't, the body of believers will be less effective.

●**12:25, 26** What is your response when a fellow Christian is honored? How do you respond when someone is suffering? We are called to rejoice with those who rejoice and weep with those who weep (Romans 12:15). Too often, unfortunately, we are jealous of those who rejoice and apathetic toward those who weep. Believers are in the world together — there is no such thing as private or individualistic Christianity. We shouldn't stop with enjoying only our own relationship with God; we need to get involved in the lives of others.

12:30 Paul discusses the subject of speaking in and interpreting tongues in more detail in chapter 14.

12:31 The greater gifts are those that are more beneficial to the body of Christ. Paul has already made it clear that one gift is not superior to another, but he urges the believers to discover how they can serve Christ's body with the gifts God has given them. Your spiritual gifts are not for your own self-advancement. They were given to you for serving God and enhancing the spiritual growth of the body of believers.

●**13:1ff** In chapter 12 Paul gave evidence of the Corinthians' lack of love in the utilization of spiritual gifts; chapter 13 defines real love; and chapter 14 shows how love works. Love is more important than all the spiritual gifts exercised in the church body. Great faith, acts of dedication or sacrifice, and miracle-working power produce very little without love. Love makes our actions and gifts

Love

And now I will show you the most excellent way.

13 If I speak in the tongues[e] of men and of angels, but have not love, I am only a resounding gong or a clanging cymbal. 2If I have the gift of prophecy and can fathom all mysteries[d] and all knowledge, and if I have a faith that can move mountains, but have not love, I am nothing. 3If I give all I possess to the poor and surrender my body to the flames,[f] but have not love, I gain nothing.

4Love is patient, love is kind. It does not envy, it does not boast, it is not proud. 5It is not rude, it is not self-seeking,[e] it is not easily angered, it keeps no record of wrongs. 6Love does not delight in evil but rejoices with the truth.[f] 7It always protects, always trusts, always hopes, always perseveres.

8Love never fails. But where there are prophecies, they will cease; where there are tongues, they will be stilled; where there is knowledge, it will pass away. 9For we know in part[g] and we prophesy in part, 10but when perfection comes,[h] the imperfect disappears. 11When I was a child, I talked like a child, I thought like a child, I reasoned like a child. When I became a man, I put childish ways behind me. 12Now we see but a poor reflection as in a mirror; then we shall see face to face.[i] Now I know in part; then I shall know fully, even as I am fully known.[j]

13And now these three remain: faith, hope and love. But the greatest of these is love.

13:2 [d]1Co 14:2
13:5 [e]1Co 10:24
13:6 [f]2Jn 4
13:9 [g]1Co 8:2
13:10 [h]Php 3:12
13:12 [i]1Jn 3:2 [j]1Co 8:3

Gifts of Prophecy and Tongues

14 Follow the way of love and eagerly desire[k] spiritual gifts, especially the gift of prophecy. 2For anyone who speaks in a tongue[g] does not speak to men but to God. Indeed, no one understands him; he utters mysteries[l] with his spirit.[h] 3But everyone who prophesies speaks to men for their strengthening, encouragement and comfort. 4He who speaks in a tongue edifies himself, but he who prophesies edifies the church. 5I would like every one of you to speak in tongues,[i] but I

14:1 [k]1Co 12:31
14:2 [l]1Co 13:2

e *1* Or *languages* f *3* Some early manuscripts *body that I may boast* g *2* Or *another language*; also in verses 4, 13, 14, 19, 26 and 27 h *2* Or *by the Spirit* i *5* Or *other languages*; also in verses 6, 18, 22, 23 and 39

---

useful. Although people have different gifts, love is available to everyone.

•**13:4–7** Our society confuses love and lust. Unlike lust, God's kind of love is directed outward toward others, not inward toward ourselves. It is utterly unselfish. This kind of love goes against our natural inclinations. It is possible to practice this love only if God helps us set aside our own desires and instincts, so that we can give love while expecting nothing in return. Thus the more we become like Christ, the more love we will show to others.

13:10 God gives us spiritual gifts for our lives on earth in order to build up, serve, and strengthen fellow Christians. The spiritual gifts are for the church. In eternity, we will be made perfect and complete and will be in the very presence of God. We will no longer need the spiritual gifts, so they will come to an end.

•**13:12** Paul offers a glimpse into the future to give us hope that one day we will be complete when we see God face to face. This truth should strengthen our faith—we don't have all the answers now, but one day we will. Someday we will see Christ in person and be able to see with God's perspective.

•**13:13** In morally corrupt Corinth, love had become a mixed-up term with little meaning. Today people are still confused about love. Love is the greatest of all human qualities, and it is an attribute of God himself (1 John 4:8). Love involves unselfish service to others; to show it gives evidence that you care. *Faith* is the foundation and content of God's message; *hope* is the attitude and focus; *love* is the action. When faith and hope are in line, you are free to love completely because you understand how God loves.

•**14:1** Prophecy may involve predicting future events, but its main purpose is to communicate God's message to people, providing insight, warning, correction, and encouragement.

•**14:2** The gift of speaking in a tongue was a concern of the Corinthian church because the use of the gift had caused disorder in worship. Speaking in tongues is a legitimate gift of the Holy Spirit, but the Corinthian believers were using it as a sign of spiritual superiority rather than as a means to spiritual unity. Spiritual gifts are beneficial only when they are properly used to help everyone in the church. We should not exercise them only to make *ourselves* feel good.

14:2ff Paul makes several points about speaking in tongues: (1) it is a spiritual gift from God (14:2); (2) it is a desirable gift even though it isn't a requirement of faith (12:28–31); (3) it is less important than prophecy and teaching (14:4). Although Paul himself spoke in tongues, he stresses prophecy (preaching) because it benefits the whole church, while speaking in tongues primarily benefits the speaker. Public worship must be understandable and edifying to the whole church.

14:5–12 As musical instruments must play each note in order for the music to be clear, so Paul says words preached in the hearers' language are more clear and helpful. There are many languages in the world (14:10), and people who speak different languages can rarely understand each other. It is the same with speaking in tongues. Although this gift is helpful to many people in private worship, and helpful in public worship with interpretation, Paul says he would rather speak five words that his hearers can understand than 10,000 that they cannot (14:19).

would rather have you prophesy.^{m} He who prophesies is greater than one who speaks in tongues,^{j} unless he interprets, so that the church may be edified.

^{m}Nu 11:29   **14:5**

^{6}Now, brothers, if I come to you and speak in tongues, what good will I be to you, unless I bring you some revelation^n or knowledge or prophecy or word of instruction? ^{7}Even in the case of lifeless things that make sounds, such as the flute or harp, how will anyone know what tune is being played unless there is a distinction in the notes? ^{8}Again, if the trumpet does not sound a clear call, who will get ready for battle?^{o} ^{9}So it is with you. Unless you speak intelligible words with your tongue, how will anyone know what you are saying? You will just be speaking into the air. ^{10}Undoubtedly there are all sorts of languages in the world, yet none of them is without meaning. ^{11}If then I do not grasp the meaning of what someone is saying, I am a foreigner to the speaker, and he is a foreigner to me. ^{12}So it is with you. Since you are eager to have spiritual gifts, try to excel in gifts that build up the church.

14:6 ^{n}ver 26

14:8 ^{o}Nu 10:9

^{13}For this reason anyone who speaks in a tongue should pray that he may interpret what he says. ^{14}For if I pray in a tongue, my spirit prays, but my mind is unfruitful. ^{15}So what shall I do? I will pray with my spirit, but I will also pray with my mind; I will sing^p with my spirit, but I will also sing with my mind. ^{16}If you are praising God with your spirit, how can one who finds himself among those who do not understand^k say "Amen"^{q} to your thanksgiving,^{r} since he does not know what you are saying? ^{17}You may be giving thanks well enough, but the other man is not edified.

14:15 ^{p}Eph 5:19

14:16 ^{q}1Ch 16:36 ^{r}1Co 11:24

^{18}I thank God that I speak in tongues more than all of you. ^{19}But in the church I would rather speak five intelligible words to instruct others than ten thousand words in a tongue.

^{20}Brothers, stop thinking like children.^{s} In regard to evil be infants,^{t} but in your thinking be adults. ^{21}In the Law^u it is written:

14:20 ^{s}Eph 4:14; Heb 5:12, 13; 1Pe 2:2 ^{t}Ro 16:19

> "Through men of strange tongues
>   and through the lips of foreigners
> I will speak to this people,
>   but even then they will not listen to me,"^{lv}

14:21 ^{u}Jn 10:34 ^{v}Isa 28:11, 12

says the Lord.

^{22}Tongues, then, are a sign, not for believers but for unbelievers; prophecy, however, is for believers, not for unbelievers. ^{23}So if the whole church comes together and everyone speaks in tongues, and some who do not understand^m or some unbelievers come in, will they not say that you are out of your mind?^{w} ^{24}But if an unbeliever or someone who does not understand^n comes in while everybody is prophesying, he will be convinced by all that he is a sinner and will be judged by all, ^{25}and the secrets of his heart will be laid bare. So he will fall down and worship God, exclaiming, "God is really among you!"^{x}

14:23 ^{w}Ac 2:13

14:25 ^{x}Isa 45:14; Zec 8:23

Orderly Worship

^{26}What then shall we say, brothers? When you come together, everyone^y has a hymn, or a word of instruction, a revelation, a tongue or an interpretation. All of

14:26 ^{y}1Co 12:7-10

^{j}5 Or *other languages*; also in verses 6, 18, 22, 23 and 39 ^{k}16 Or *among the inquirers* ^{l}21 Isaiah 28:11,12 ^{m}23 Or *some inquirers* ^{n}24 Or *or some inquirer*

14:13-20 If a person has the gift of speaking in tongues, he should also pray for the gift of knowing what he has said (interpretation) so he can tell people afterwards. This way, the entire church will be edified by this gift.

14:15 There is a proper place for the intellect in Christianity. In praying and singing, both the mind and the spirit are to be fully engaged. When we sing, we should also think about the meaning of the words. When we pour out our feelings to God in prayer, we should not turn off our capacity to think. True Christianity is neither barren intellectualism nor thoughtless emotionalism. See also Ephesians 1:17, 18; Philippians 1:9–11; Colossians 1:9.

● **14:22-25** The way the Corinthians were speaking in tongues was helping no one because believers did not understand what was being said, and unbelievers thought that the people speaking in tongues were crazy. Speaking in tongues was supposed to be a *sign* to unbelievers (as it was in Acts 2). After speaking in tongues, believers were supposed to explain what was said and give the credit to God. The unsaved people would then be convinced of a spiritual reality and motivated to look further into the Christian faith. While this is one way to reach unbelievers, Paul says that clear preaching is usually better (14:5).

● **14:26ff** Everything done in worship services must be beneficial to

these must be done for the strengthening of the church. 27If anyone speaks in a tongue, two — or at the most three — should speak, one at a time, and someone must interpret. 28If there is no interpreter, the speaker should keep quiet in the church and speak to himself and God.

29Two or three prophets should speak, and the others should weigh carefully what is said. z 30And if a revelation comes to someone who is sitting down, the first speaker should stop. 31For you can all prophesy in turn so that everyone may be instructed and encouraged. 32The spirits of prophets are subject to the control of prophets. 33For God is not a God of disorder but of peace.

As in all the congregations of the saints, 34women should remain silent in the churches. They are not allowed to speak, but must be in submission,a as the Law says. 35If they want to inquire about something, they should ask their own husbands at home; for it is disgraceful for a woman to speak in the church.

36Did the word of God originate with you? Or are you the only people it has reached? 37If anybody thinks he is a prophetb or spiritually gifted, let him acknowledge that what I am writing to you is the Lord's command.c 38If he ignores this, he himself will be ignored.o

39Therefore, my brothers, be eagerd to prophesy, and do not forbid speaking in tongues. 40But everything should be done in a fitting and orderlye way.

4. Instruction on the resurrection
The Resurrection of Christ

15 Now, brothers, I want to remind you of the gospel I preached to you, which you received and on which you have taken your stand. 2By this gospel you are saved, if you hold firmly to the word I preached to you. Otherwise, you have believed in vain.

3For what I received I passed on to you as of first importancep: that Christ died for our sinsf according to the Scriptures,g 4that he was buried, that he was raised on the third day according to the Scriptures,h 5and that he appeared to Peter,qi and then to the Twelve. 6After that, he appeared to more than five hundred of the brothers at the same time, most of whom are still living, though some have fallen

o 38 Some manuscripts *If he is ignorant of this, let him be ignorant* p 3 Or *you at the first* q 5 Greek *Cephas*

Margin references:

14:29
z 1Co 12:10

14:34
a 1Ti 2:11, 12

14:37
b 2Co 10:7
c 1Jn 4:6

14:39
d 1Co 12:31

14:40
e ver 33

15:3
f Isa 53:5;
1Pe 2:24
g Lk 24:27;
Ac 26:22, 23

15:4
h Ac 2:25, 30, 31

15:5
i Lk 24:34

---

the worshipers. This principle touches every aspect — singing, preaching, and the exercise of spiritual gifts. Those contributing to the service (singers, speakers, readers) must have love as their chief motivation, speaking useful words or participating in a way that will strengthen the faith of other believers.

●**14:33** In worship, everything must be done in harmony and with order. Even when the gifts of the Holy Spirit are being exercised, there is no excuse for disorder. When there is chaos, the church is not allowing God to work among believers as he would like.

14:34, 35 Does this mean that women should not speak in church services today? It is clear from 11:5 that women prayed and prophesied in public worship. It is also clear in chapters 12 – 14 that women are given spiritual gifts and are encouraged to exercise them in the body of Christ. Women have much to contribute and can participate in worship services.

In the Corinthian culture, women were not allowed to confront men in public. Apparently some of the women who had become Christians thought that their Christian freedom gave them the right to question the men in public worship. This was causing division in the church. In addition, women of that day did not receive formal religious education as did the men. Women may have been raising questions in the worship services that could have been answered at home without disrupting the services. Paul was asking the women not to flaunt their Christian freedom during worship. The purpose of Paul's words was to promote unity, not to teach about women's role in the church.

14:40 Worship is vital to the life of an individual and to the whole church. Our church services should be conducted in an orderly way so that we can worship, be taught, and be prepared to serve God. Those who are responsible for planning worship should make sure it has order and direction rather than chaos and confusion.

15:2 Most churches contain people who do not yet believe. Some are moving in the direction of belief, and others are simply pretending. Imposters, however, are not to be removed (see Matthew 13:28, 29), for that is the Lord's work alone. The Good News about Jesus Christ will save us *if* we firmly believe it and faithfully follow it.

●**15:5-8** There will always be people who say that Jesus didn't rise from the dead. Paul assures us that many people saw Jesus after his resurrection: Peter; the disciples (the Twelve); more than 500 Christian believers (most of whom were still alive when Paul wrote this, although some had died); James (Jesus' brother); all the apostles; and finally Paul himself. The resurrection is an historical fact. Don't be discouraged by doubters who deny the resurrection. Be filled with hope because of the knowledge that one day you, and they, will see the living proof when Christ returns. (For more evidence on the resurrection, see the chart in Mark 16.)

asleep. 7Then he appeared to James, then to all the apostles,ⁱ 8and last of all he appeared to me also,ᵏ as to one abnormally born.

9For I am the least of the apostlesˡ and do not even deserve to be called an apostle, because I persecutedᵐ the church of God. 10But by the grace of God I am what I am, and his grace to me was not without effect. No, I worked harder than all of themⁿ — yet not I, but the grace of God that was with me.ᵒ 11Whether, then, it was I or they, this is what we preach, and this is what you believed.

The Resurrection of the Dead

12But if it is preached that Christ has been raised from the dead, how can some of you say that there is no resurrection of the dead? 13If there is no resurrection of the dead, then not even Christ has been raised. 14And if Christ has not been raised, our preaching is useless and so is your faith. 15More than that, we are then found to be false witnesses about God, for we have testified about God that he raised Christ from the dead.ᵖ But he did not raise him if in fact the dead are not raised. 16For if the dead are not raised, then Christ has not been raised either. 17And if Christ has not been raised, your faith is futile; you are still in your sins. 18Then those also who have fallen asleep in Christ are lost. 19If only for this life we have hope in Christ, we are to be pitied more than all men.

20But Christ has indeed been raised from the dead,ۑ the firstfruitsʳ of those who have fallen asleep. 21For since death came through a man,ˢ the resurrection of the dead comes also through a man. 22For as in Adam all die, so in Christ all will be made alive. 23But each in his own turn: Christ, the firstfruits; then, when he comes, those who belong to him. 24Then the end will come, when he hands over the kingdomᵗ to God the Father after he has destroyed all dominion, authority and power. 25For he must reign until he has put all his enemies under his feet. 26The last enemy

15:7 /Ac 1:3, 4
15:8 ᵏAc 9:3-6, 17
15:9 ˡEph 3:8 ᵐAc 8:3
15:10 ⁿ2Co 11:23 ᵒPhp 2:13
15:15 ᵖAc 2:24
15:20 ۑ1Pe 1:3 ʳAc 26:23
15:21 ˢRo 5:12
15:24 ᵗDa 7:14, 27

15:7 This James is Jesus' brother, who at first did not believe that Jesus was the Messiah (John 7:5). After seeing the resurrected Christ, he became a believer and ultimately a leader of the church in Jerusalem (Acts 15:13). James wrote the New Testament book of James.

15:8, 9 Paul's most important credential to be an apostle was that he was an eyewitness of the risen Christ (see Acts 9:3–6). "Abnormally born" means that his was a special case. The other apostles saw Christ in the flesh. Paul was in the next generation of believers — yet Christ appeared to him.

15:9, 10 As a zealous Pharisee, Paul had been an enemy of the Christian church — even to the point of capturing and persecuting believers (see Acts 9:1–3). Thus he felt unworthy to be called an apostle of Christ. Though undoubtedly the most influential of the apostles, Paul was deeply humble. He knew that he had worked hard and accomplished much, but only because God had poured kindness and grace upon him. True humility is not convincing yourself that you are worthless, but recognizing God's work in you. It is having God's perspective on who you are and acknowledging his grace in developing your abilities.

15:10 Paul wrote of working harder than the other apostles. This was not an arrogant boast because he knew that his power came from God and that it really didn't matter who worked hardest. Because of his prominent position as a Pharisee, Paul's conversion made him the object of even greater persecution than the other apostles; thus he had to work harder to preach the same message.

●**15:12ff** Most Greeks did not believe that people's bodies would be resurrected after death. They saw the afterlife as something that happened only to the soul. According to Greek philosophers, the soul was the real person, imprisoned in a physical body, and at death the soul was released. There was no immortality for the body, but the soul entered an eternal state. Christianity, by contrast, affirms that the body and soul will be united after resurrection. The church at Corinth was in the heart of Greek culture. Thus many believers had a difficult time believing in a bodily resurrec-

tion. Paul wrote this part of his letter to clear up this confusion about the resurrection.

●**15:13–18** The resurrection of Christ is the center of the Christian faith. Because Christ rose from the dead as he promised, we know that what he said is true — he is God. Because he rose, we have certainty that our sins are forgiven. Because he rose, he lives and represents us to God. Because he rose and defeated death, we know we will also be raised.

●**15:19** Why does Paul say believers should be pitied if there were only earthly value to Christianity? In Paul's day, Christianity often brought a person persecution, ostracism from family, and, in many cases, poverty. There were few tangible benefits from being a Christian in that society. It was certainly not a step up the social or career ladder. Even more important, however, is the fact that if Christ had not been resurrected from death, Christians would not be forgiven for their sins and would have no hope of eternal life.

15:20 Firstfruits were the first part of the harvest that faithful Jews brought to the temple as an offering (Leviticus 23:10ff). Although Christ was not the first to rise from the dead (he raised Lazarus and others), he was the first to never die again. He is the forerunner for us, the proof of our eventual resurrection to eternal life.

15:21 Death came into the world as a result of Adam and Eve's sin. In Romans 5:12–21, Paul explained why Adam's sin brought sin to all people, how death and sin spread to all humans because of this first sin, and the parallel between Adam's death and Christ's death.

15:24–28 This is not a chronological sequence of events, and no specific time for these events is given. Paul's point is that the resurrected Christ will conquer all evil, including death. See Revelation 20:14 for words about the final destruction of death.

15:25–28 Although God the Father and God the Son are equal, each has a special work to do and an area of sovereign control (15:28). Christ is not inferior to the Father, but his work is to defeat all evil on earth. First he defeated sin and death on the cross, and in the final days, he will defeat Satan and all evil. World events may

15:26
u Rev 20:14

15:27
v Ps 8:6

15:28
w Php 3:21
x 1Co 3:23

15:30
y 2Co 11:26

15:32
z 2Co 1:8
a Lk 12:19

15:35
b Eze 37:3

15:36
c Jn 12:24

15:42
d Mt 13:43

15:43
e Php 3:21

to be destroyed is death. u 27For he "has put everything under his feet."r v Now when it says that "everything" has been put under him, it is clear that this does not include God himself, who put everything under Christ. 28When he has done this, then the Son himself will be made subject to him who put everything under him, w so that God may be all in all. x

29Now if there is no resurrection, what will those do who are baptized for the dead? If the dead are not raised at all, why are people baptized for them? 30And as for us, why do we endanger ourselves every hour?y 31I die every day—I mean that, brothers—just as surely as I glory over you in Christ Jesus our Lord. 32If I fought wild beastsz in Ephesus for merely human reasons, what have I gained? If the dead are not raised,

"Let us eat and drink,
for tomorrow we die."s a

33Do not be misled: "Bad company corrupts good character." 34Come back to your senses as you ought, and stop sinning; for there are some who are ignorant of God—I say this to your shame.

The Resurrection Body

35But someone may ask, "How are the dead raised? With what kind of body will they come?"b 36How foolish! What you sow does not come to life unless it dies. c 37When you sow, you do not plant the body that will be, but just a seed, perhaps of wheat or of something else. 38But God gives it a body as he has determined, and to each kind of seed he gives its own body. 39All flesh is not the same: Men have one kind of flesh, animals have another, birds another and fish another. 40There are also heavenly bodies and there are earthly bodies; but the splendor of the heavenly bodies is one kind, and the splendor of the earthly bodies is another. 41The sun has one kind of splendor, the moon another and the stars another; and star differs from star in splendor.

42So will it bed with the resurrection of the dead. The body that is sown is perishable, it is raised imperishable; 43it is sown in dishonor, it is raised in glory;e it is sown in weakness, it is raised in power; 44it is sown a natural body, it is raised a spiritual body.

r 27 Psalm 8:6   s 32 Isaiah 22:13

---

seem out of control and justice may seem scarce. But God is in control, allowing evil to remain for a time until he sends Jesus to earth again. Then Christ will present to God a perfect new world.

15:29 Some believers were baptized on behalf of others who had died unbaptized. Nothing more is known about this practice, but it obviously affirms a belief in resurrection. Paul is not promoting baptism for the dead; he is illustrating his argument that the resurrection is a reality.

●**15:30–34** If death ended it all, enjoying the moment would be all that matters. But Christians know that there is life beyond the grave and that our life on earth is only a preparation for our life that will never end. What you do today matters for eternity. In light of eternity, sin is a foolish gamble.

15:31, 32 "I die every day" refers to Paul's daily exposure to danger. There is no evidence that Paul actually "fought wild beasts in Ephesus," but rather he was referring to the savage opposition he had faced.

15:33 Keeping company with those who deny the resurrection could corrupt good Christian character. Don't let your relationships with unbelievers lead you away from Christ or cause your faith to waver.

15:35ff Paul launches into a discussion about what our resurrected bodies will be like. If you could select your own body, what

kind would you choose—strong, athletic, beautiful? Paul explains that we will be recognized in our resurrected bodies, yet they will be better than we can imagine, for they will be made to live forever. We will still have our own personalities and individualities, but these will be perfected through Christ's work. The Bible does not reveal everything that our resurrected bodies will be able to do, but we know they will be perfect, without sickness or disease (see Philippians 3:21).

●**15:35ff** Paul compares the resurrection of our bodies with the growth in a garden. Seeds placed in the ground don't grow unless they "die" first. The plant that grows looks very different from the seed because God gives it a new "body." There are different kinds of bodies—people, animals, fish, birds. Even the angels in heaven have bodies that are different in beauty and glory. Our resurrected bodies will be very different in some ways, but not all, from our earthly bodies.

●**15:42–44** Our present bodies are perishable and prone to decay. Our resurrection bodies will be transformed. These spiritual bodies will not be limited by the laws of nature. This does not necessarily mean we'll be superpeople, but our bodies will be different from and more capable than our present earthly bodies. Our spiritual bodies will not be weak, will never get sick, and will never die.

If there is a natural body, there is also a spiritual body. 45So it is written: "The first man Adam became a living being"t;f the last Adam,g a life-giving spirit. 46The spiritual did not come first, but the natural, and after that the spiritual. 47The first man was of the dust of the earth,h the second man from heaven. 48As was the earthly man, so are those who are of the earth; and as is the man from heaven, so also are those who are of heaven. 49And just as we have borne the likeness of the earthly man,i so shall weu bear the likeness of the man from heaven.j

50I declare to you, brothers, that flesh and blood cannot inherit the kingdom of God, nor does the perishable inherit the imperishable. 51Listen, I tell you a mystery: We will not all sleep, but we will all be changed— 52in a flash, in the twinkling of an eye, at the last trumpet. For the trumpet will sound,k the dead will be raised imperishable, and we will be changed. 53For the perishable must clothe itself with the imperishable,l and the mortal with immortality. 54When the perishable has been clothed with the imperishable, and the mortal with immortality, then the saying that is written will come true: "Death has been swallowed up in victory."vm

55"Where, O death, is your victory?
Where, O death, is your sting?"wn

56The sting of death is sin, and the power of sin is the law.o 57But thanks be to God! He gives us the victory through our Lord Jesus Christ.

58Therefore, my dear brothers, stand firm. Let nothing move you. Always give yourselves fully to the work of the Lord, because you know that your labor in the Lord is not in vain.

The Collection for God's People

16 Now about the collectionp for God's people:q Do what I told the Galatian churches to do. 2On the first day of every week,r each one of you should set aside a sum of money in keeping with his income, saving it up, so that when I come no collections will have to be made. 3Then, when I arrive, I will give letters of introduction to the men you approve and send them with your gift to Jerusalem. 4If it seems advisable for me to go also, they will accompany me.

t 45 Gen. 2:7 u 49 Some early manuscripts so let us v 54 Isaiah 25:8 w 55 Hosea 13:14

15:45 fGe 2:7 gRo 5:14
15:47 hGe 3:19
15:49 iGe 5:3 jRo 8:29
15:52 kMt 24:31
15:53 l2Co 5:2, 4
15:54 mIsa 25:8
15:55 nHos 13:14
15:56 oRo 4:15
16:1 pAc 24:17 qAc 9:13
16:2 rAc 20:7

●**15:45** The "last Adam" refers to Christ. Because Christ rose from the dead, he is a life-giving spirit. This means that he entered into a new form of existence (see the note on 2 Corinthians 3:17). He is the source of the spiritual life that will result in our resurrection. Christ's new glorified human body now suits his new glorified life—just as Adam's human body was suitable to his natural life. When we are resurrected, God will give us a transformed, eternal body suited to our new eternal life.

15:50–53 We all face limitations. Those who have physical, mental, or emotional disabilities are especially aware of this. Some may be blind, but they can see a new way to live. Some may be deaf, but they can hear God's Good News. Some may be lame, but they can walk in God's love. In addition, they have the encouragement that those disabilities are only temporary. Paul tells us that we all will be given new bodies when Christ returns and that these bodies will be without disabilities, never to die or become sick. This can give us hope in our suffering.

15:51, 52 "We will not all sleep" means that Christians alive at that day will not have to die but will be transformed immediately. A trumpet blast will usher in the new heaven and earth. The Jews would understand the significance of this because trumpets were always blown to signal the start of great festivals and other extraordinary events (Numbers 10:10).

15:54–56 Satan seemed to be victorious in the Garden of Eden (Genesis 3) and at the cross of Jesus. But God turned Satan's apparent victory into defeat when Jesus Christ rose from the dead (Colossians 2:15; Hebrews 2:14, 15). Thus death is no longer a source of dread or fear. Christ overcame it, and one day we will also. The law will no longer make sinners out of us who cannot keep it. Death has been defeated, and we have hope beyond the grave.

●**15:58** Paul says that because of the resurrection, nothing we do is in vain. Sometimes we hesitate to do good because we don't see any results. But if we can maintain a heavenly perspective, we will understand that we often will not see the good that results from our efforts. If we truly believe that Christ has won the ultimate victory, that fact must affect the way we live right now. Don't let discouragement over an apparent lack of results keep you from working. Do the good that you have opportunity to do, knowing that your work will have eternal results.

16:1ff Paul had just said that no good deed is ever in vain (15:58). In this chapter he mentions some practical deeds that have value for all Christians.

●**16:1–4** The Christians in Jerusalem were suffering from poverty and famine, so Paul was collecting money for them (Romans 15:25–31; 2 Corinthians 8:4; 9:1ff). He suggested that believers set aside a certain amount each week and give it to the church until he arrived to take it on to Jerusalem. Paul had planned to go straight to Corinth from Ephesus, but he changed his mind (2 Corinthians 1; 2). When he finally arrived, he took the gift and delivered it to the Jerusalem church (Acts 21:18; 24:17).

Personal Requests

5After I go through Macedonia, I will come to you — for I will be going through Macedonia. 6Perhaps I will stay with you awhile, or even spend the winter, so that you can help me on my journey, wherever I go. 7I do not want to see you now and make only a passing visit; I hope to spend some time with you, if the Lord permits. *s* 8But I will stay on at Ephesus until Pentecost, 9because a great door for effective work has opened to me, and there are many who oppose me.

10If Timothy *t* comes, see to it that he has nothing to fear while he is with you, for he is carrying on the work of the Lord, *u* just as I am. 11No one, then, should refuse to accept him. *v* Send him on his way in peace *w* so that he may return to me. I am expecting him along with the brothers.

12Now about our brother Apollos: I strongly urged him to go to you with the brothers. He was quite unwilling to go now, but he will go when he has the opportunity.

13Be on your guard; stand firm *x* in the faith; be men of courage; be strong. *y* 14Do everything in love.

15You know that the household of Stephanas were the first converts in Achaia, and they have devoted themselves to the service of the saints. I urge you, brothers, 16to submit to such as these and to everyone who joins in the work, and labors at it. 17I was glad when Stephanas, Fortunatus and Achaicus arrived, because they have supplied what was lacking from you. *z* 18For they refreshed my spirit and yours also. Such men deserve recognition. *a*

Final Greetings

19The churches in the province of Asia send you greetings. Aquila and Priscilla*x* greet you warmly in the Lord, and so does the church that meets at their house. *b* 20All the brothers here send you greetings. Greet one another with a holy kiss.

x *19* Greek *Prisca*, a variant of *Priscilla*

16:7 *s* Ac 18:21

16:10 *t* Ac 16:1 *u* 1Co 15:58

16:11 *v* 1Ti 4:12 *w* Ac 15:33

16:13 *x* Php 1:27 *y* Eph 6:10

16:17 *z* 2Co 11:9

16:18 *a* Php 2:29

16:19 *b* Ro 16:5

PHYSICAL AND RESURRECTION BODIES

Physical Bodies	Resurrection Bodies
Perishable	Imperishable
Sown in dishonor	Raised in glory
Sown in weakness	Raised in power
Natural	Spiritual
From the dust	From heaven

We all have bodies—each looks different, each has different strengths and weaknesses. But as physical, earthly bodies, they are all alike. All believers are promised life after death and bodies like Christ's (15:49), resurrection bodies.

16:10, 11 Paul was sending Timothy ahead to Corinth. Paul respected Timothy and had worked closely with him (Philippians 2:22; 1 Timothy 1:2). Although Timothy was young, Paul encouraged the Corinthian church to welcome him because he was doing the Lord's work. God's work is not limited by age. Paul wrote two personal letters to Timothy that have been preserved in the Bible (1 and 2 Timothy).

16:12 Apollos, who had preached in Corinth, was doing evangelistic work in Greece (see Acts 18:24–28; 1 Corinthians 3:3ff). Apollos didn't go to Corinth right away, partly because he knew of the factions there and didn't want to cause any more divisions.

●**16:13, 14** As the Corinthians awaited Paul's next visit, they were directed to (1) be on their guard against spiritual dangers, (2) stand firm in the faith, (3) behave courageously, (4) be strong, and (5) do everything with kindness and in love. Today, as we wait for the return of Christ, we should follow the same instructions.

●**16:19** Aquila and Priscilla were tentmakers (or leather workers) whom Paul had met in Corinth (Acts 18:1–3). They followed Paul to Ephesus and lived there with him, helping to teach others about Jesus (Romans 16:3–5). Many in the Corinthian church would have known this Christian couple. They are also mentioned in Acts 18:18, 26; Romans 16:3; 2 Timothy 4:19.

16:20 Kissing was a normal way of greeting each other in Paul's day. Paul encouraged the "holy kiss" as a way to greet Christians, and a way to help break down the divisions in this church.

16:21 Paul had a helper, or secretary, who wrote down this letter while he dictated. Paul wrote the final words, however, in his own handwriting. This is similar to adding a handwritten postscript (P.S.) to a typewritten letter. It also served to verify that this was a genuine letter from the apostle, and not a forgery.

●**16:22** The Lord Jesus Christ is coming back to earth again. To Paul, this was a glad hope, the very best he could look forward to. He was not afraid of seeing Christ — he could hardly wait! Do you share Paul's eager anticipation? Those who love Christ are looking forward to that wonderful time of his return (Titus 2:13). To those who did not love the Lord, however, Paul says, let them be cursed.

21I, Paul, write this greeting in my own hand.
22If anyone does not love the Lord*c* — a curse be on him. Come, O Lord*y*!
23The grace of the Lord Jesus be with you. *d*
24My love to all of you in Christ Jesus. Amen. *z*

16:22
c Eph 6:24

16:23
d Ro 16:20

y 22 In Aramaic the expression *Come, O Lord* is *Marana tha.*   *z 24* Some manuscripts do not have *Amen.*

● **16:24** The church at Corinth was a church in trouble. Paul lovingly and forcefully confronted their problems and pointed them back to Christ. He dealt with divisions and conflicts, selfishness, inconsiderate use of freedom, disorder in worship, misuse of spiritual gifts, and wrong attitudes about the resurrection.

In every church, there are enough problems to create tensions and divisions. We should not ignore or gloss over problems in our churches or in our lives. Instead, like Paul, we should deal with problems head on as they arise. The lesson for us in 1 Corinthians is that unity and love in a church are far more important than leaders and labels.

STUDY QUESTIONS

Thirteen lessons for individual or group study

It's always exciting to get more than you expect. And that's what you'll find in this Bible study guide—much more than you expect. Our goal was to write thoughtful, practical, dependable, and application-oriented studies of God's Word.

This study guide contains the complete text of the selected Bible book. The commentary is accurate, complete, and loaded with unique charts, maps, and profiles of Bible people.

With the Bible text, extensive notes and helps, and questions to guide discussion, these Life Application study guides have everything you need in one place.

The lessons in this Bible study guide will work for large classes as well as small group studies. To get everyone involved in your discussions, encourage participants to answer the questions before each meeting.

Each lesson is divided into five easy-to-lead sections. The section called "Reflect" introduces you and the members of your group to a specific area of life touched by the lesson. "Read" shows which chapters to read and which notes and other features to use. Additional questions help you understand the passage. "Realize" brings into focus the biblical principle to be learned with questions, a special insight, or both. "Respond" helps you make connections with your own situation and personal needs. The questions are designed to help you find areas in your life where you can apply the biblical truths. "Resolve" helps you map out action plans for that day.

Begin and end each lesson with prayer, asking for the Holy Spirit's guidance, direction, and wisdom.

Recommended time allotments for each section of a lesson:

Segment	60 minutes	90 minutes
Reflect on your life	5 minutes	10 minutes
Read the passage	10 minutes	15 minutes
Realize the principle	15 minutes	20 minutes
Respond to the message	20 minutes	30 minutes
Resolve to take action	10 minutes	15 minutes

All five sections work together to help a person learn the lessons, live out the principles, and obey the commands taught in the Bible.

Also, at the end of each lesson, there is a section entitled "More for studying other themes in this section." These questions will help you lead the group in studying other parts of each section not covered in depth by the main lesson.

Do not merely listen to the word, and so deceive yourselves. Do what it says. Anyone who listens to the word but does not do what it says is like a man who looks at his face in a mirror and, after looking at himself, goes away and immediately forgets what he looks like. But the man who looks intently into the perfect law that gives freedom, and continues to do this, not forgetting what he has heard, but doing it—he will be blessed in what he does. (James 1:22-25, NIV)

REFLECT
on your life

1 What's the best church you ever attended? What made it such a good church?

_____

_____

_____

_____

_____

2 What were some of the problems this church faced?

_____

_____

_____

_____

_____

READ
the passage

Read the Introduction to 1 Corinthians, the map "Corinth and Ephesus" (chapter 1), 1 Corinthians 1:1-9, and the following notes:

❑1:1 ❑1:2 ❑1:3 ❑1:7 ❑1:7-9

3 Why did Paul write this letter to the church in Corinth?

_____

_____

_____

_____

4 What was the city of Corinth like?

_____

_____

_____

_____

5 Why did Paul begin his letter with such a positive opening?

_____

_____

_____

_____

6 List five problems that Paul wrote about in 1 Corinthians. Which of these are of interest to you?

_____

_____

_____

_____

_____

7 Paul reminded the Corinthians of what God had done for them in the past (1:4-9). What are the benefits of remembering God's work in your life and in the work of your church?

REALIZE
the principle

_____

_____

_____

The first-century church was far from ideal, especially in Corinth. Pressured by a pagan culture, the Christians there were divided by conflicts and immorality. Though the church at Corinth was gifted, it was spiritually immature. In many ways, it was like some young churches today. Problems brought discouragement. Paul wrote to this church to bring them hope and to confront the problems plaguing them. They needed to change, and God was able to help them. We need those same reminders in our churches and personal lives.

8 What problems do churches today have that are similar to those faced by the Corinthian church in the first century?

_____

_____

_____

_____

_____

_____

_____

_____

9 What are some twentieth-century problems that churches encounter today?

_____

_____

_____

_____

_____

_____

_____

RESPOND
to the message

10 If Paul were to address a letter to your church, what might he commend?

_____

_____

_____

_____

_____

11 What would he want to correct?

_____

_____

_____

_____

12 What can you do about the problems confronting your church?

_____

_____

_____

_____

_____

13 Pray each day this week for your church. Ask God what you can do to help strengthen your church. What leaders and others can you pray for?

_____

_____

_____

_____

_____

RESOLVE
to take action

A Besides the Corinthians, to whom does this letter apply (1:2)? Which of the needs of the Corinthian church are needs in your church?

B What were some of the good qualities of the Corinthian church (1:2-9)? Where did they get these qualities? What good qualities does your church have?

C Why did the Corinthians "eagerly wait for our Lord Jesus Christ to be revealed" (1:7)? What does this mean for you? How does it apply to your responsibilities and commitments?

D What could the Corinthian Christians count on (1:8, 9)? How might this assurance affect a Christian? How does it affect you?

MORE
for studying
other themes
in this section

REFLECT
on your life

1 List two or three common wise sayings or aphorisms (for example, "A penny saved is a penny earned").

_____

_____

_____

_____

2 What is one of your favorite wise sayings?

_____

_____

_____

_____

READ
the passage

Read 1 Corinthians 1:10—2:16 and the following notes:

❏1:19 ❏1:22-24 ❏1:25 ❏2:4 ❏2:7 ❏2:10 ❏2:14, 15

3 What is foolish about the message of the cross (1:21-28)?

_____

_____

_____

_____

4 Why has God chosen what the world considers foolish (1:29-31)?

_____

_____

_____

_____

_____

5 In what ways were the Corinthians thinking with the world's mind and not with the mind of Christ?

_____

_____

_____

_____

_____

6 For what reasons do many people today consider the message of the cross to be foolish?

_____

_____

_____

_____

REALIZE
the principle

Conventional wisdom says that changing the world requires eloquent spokes-persons, popular leaders, and the use of power. Instead, God used ordinary, humble, and powerless people. And most amazing of all, he used the cross. Who would expect a Savior to die as a criminal? No wonder God's ways seem foolish to the world. The problem in the Corinthian church was that people were still looking at life from the world's perspective. This led to popularity contests, divisions, and spiritual pride. Paul had to bring them back to reality.

7 Why is it important to live God's way and not the world's?

_____

_____

_____

_____

8 Why doesn't the world doesn't understand God's ways?

_____

_____

_____

_____

9 What are some examples of God's values conflicting with your culture's values?

_____

_____

_____

_____

10 What makes it difficult to live by God's wisdom and reject the world's wisdom?

_____

_____

_____

_____

RESPOND
to the message

11 In what areas are Christians tempted to have the world's values?

_____

_____

_____

_____

12 Where in your own life does this battle occur?

_____

_____

_____

_____

13 How do you tell the difference between God's wisdom and the world's wisdom?

_____

_____

_____

_____

14 Write down at least one area in your life where you have been listening to the world more than God.

_____

_____

_____

_____

RESOLVE
to take action

15 How would God's wisdom change your situation?

_____

_____

_____

_____

16 What new, first step in following God's wisdom could you take within the next week?

_____

_____

_____

_____

A In what ways would the message of Christ seem foolish to a Jewish person? What unique issues might need to be addressed in explaining the gospel to him/her?

MORE
for studying
other themes
in this section

B How did Paul approach ministry (2:1-5)? What lessons does this have for anyone in ministry today?

C What does it mean to have the mind of Christ (2:16)? How does Paul's assurance that we have the mind of Christ affect you?

D What is "God's secret wisdom" (2:7)? How can a person have this wisdom?

REFLECT
on your life

1 List as many different church denominations as you can think of.

_____

_____

_____

_____

_____

_____

2 How did we end up with so many different kinds of churches?

_____

_____

_____

_____

READ
the passage

Read 1 Corinthians 3:1—4:21 and the following notes:

☑3:6 ☑3:10, 11 ☑3:10-17 ☑3:13-15 ☑4:1, 2 ☑4:6, 7 ☑4:15

3 What situation in the church was Paul addressing (3:1-4)?

_____

_____

4 What were some of the reasons for this situation (1:3-4)?

_____

_____

_____

_____

5 Why was this troubling to Paul (3:1-9)?

_____

_____

_____

_____

6 How did Paul address this problem? (See 3:8-10; 4:6, 7.)

_____

_____

_____

_____

7 Why do you think Paul placed such an emphasis on his life-style and apostle-ship in this passage of Scripture?

REALIZE
the principle

_____

_____

_____

_____

Paul spoke to the Corinthians as their spiritual father. He had a pure and genuine concern for their welfare and spiritual growth, but he saw the young church being split into factions around personalities and leadership styles. Because people were taking such pride in the groups they belonged to, the church was divided. It's good and normal to appreciate gifted people and to follow spiritual leaders, but when that appreciation leads to feelings of superiority, arrogance, or pride, the church is weakened and the Lord saddened. As you look around at other groups, both inside and outside your church, be appreciative of differences. Thank God if you are someplace where your needs are being met and you are growing in Christ. But remember the simple truth that there is only one foundation, Jesus Christ, and that all we have or do comes from him. Watch out for the natural tendency to take sides.

8 What does it mean that Jesus Christ is the foundation (3:11)? How do we build on this foundation?

_____

_____

_____

_____

RESPOND
to the message

9 What kinds of things are "gold, silver, costly stones"? What kinds of things are "wood, hay or straw" (3:12)?

_____

_____

_____

_____

_____

10 In your experience, what are some of the main causes of divisions and splits in churches?

_____

_____

_____

_____

11 When can appreciation for a leader become a problem?

_____

_____

_____

_____

12 In your church, what are some of the potential (or existing) causes of division?

_____

_____

_____

_____

13 What are some ways to promote unity in your church, either to prevent divisions or help heal the ones that exist?

_____

_____

_____

_____

14 Ask God to use you to promote unity in your church. Write a one or two sentence statement that expresses your determination to do so.

_____

_____

_____

_____

RESOLVE
to take action

15 Write down the names of the leaders in your church (or other spiritual leaders you follow) for whom you will pray this week. Ask God to use them but to protect them from the temptations of power and pride.

_____

_____

_____

_____

A Discuss the relationship between faith and deeds in the Christian life. What incentives are found in this passage for being a wise worker (builder)? What kind of a house are you building?

MORE
for studying
other themes
in this section

B In what ways will we be rewarded in heaven for our obedience and faithfulness (3:8, 13-15)?

C What would it have been like to be an apostle? In what ways does God call you to similar experiences?

D Why did Paul urge people to live as he lived? In what ways would you want people to imitate you?

REFLECT
on your life

1 What kinds of disciplinary methods did your parents use when you were a child?

_____

_____

_____

2 What disciplinary methods did they use when you were in high school?

_____

_____

_____

3 What is the purpose of discipline?

_____

_____

_____

_____

4 What instructions did Paul give to resolve the immoral situation described in 1 Corinthians 5?

_____

_____

_____

_____

_____

_____

5 What is the purpose of church discipline (5:5)?

_____

_____

_____

_____

6 What does the phrase "hand this man over to Satan" mean (5:5)?

_____

_____

_____

_____

_____

People sometimes think of church discipline as negative and unloving. But when applied as the Bible describes, it can be an instrument of healing and forgiveness. Paul taught the Corinthian believers to use discipline to keep the church pure and to bring wayward members back to Christ. We need such discipline because it is easy to gloss over sin in our life and in the church. Sin needs to be dealt with so it will not gain a foothold.

REALIZE
the principle

7 Why is purity such a vital issue for a Christian and for the church?

_____

_____

_____

8 What role does church discipline have in the Christian's call to purity?

_____

_____

_____

_____

9 Since each Christian struggles with sin every day, what determines when church discipline is appropriate?

_____

_____

_____

_____

_____

_____

RESPOND
to the message

10 How would you feel if someone approached you with a rebuke or correction? What would be your response?

_____

_____

_____

_____

_____

_____

11 What stages of church discipline can all Christians be a part of? (See the chart "Church Discipline.")

_____

_____

_____

_____

12 How can being accountable to others help a person remain pure?

_____

_____

_____

_____

_____

13 In what ways is it possible to honor God with your body?

_____

_____

_____

_____

14 Who knows you well enough to hold you accountable for a life-style of purity? When could you talk to that person about a mutual agreement to pray for each other and be open with each other about purity issues?

_____

_____

_____

_____

_____

RESOLVE
to take action

15 Pray for your church to be a place that encourages and promotes Biblical purity.

A Paul gave instructions on lawsuits between Christians (6:1-8). How should Christians settle their disputes? Why is it important for Christians not to go to court against one another? To what extent should a Christian go to avoid taking another Christian to court?

B What does it mean that our body is the "temple of the Holy Spirit" (6:19)? In what ways does this influence your behavior?

C What is so harmful about sexual immorality? How does our culture make it difficult for people to remain sexually pure? What can we do to counteract those influences?

MORE
for studying
other themes
in this section

REFLECT
on your life

1 Give an example of when people might think, *The grass is greener on the other side of the fence.*

_____

_____

_____

_____

_____

2 How might married and single people think this way?

_____

_____

_____

_____

READ
the passage

Read 1 Corinthians 7:1-40 and the following notes:

☐7:3-11 ☐7:4 ☐7:7 ☐7:12-14 ☐7:20 ☐7:28

3 What are the different life situations addressed in this chapter? (7:1-40)

_____

_____

_____

_____

4 What are the advantages of remaining single? (See 7:7-8, 24, 28, 32-34, 36-38.)

_____

_____

_____

_____

5 What are the advantages of being married? (See 7:7, 9, 24, 36-38.)

_____

_____

_____

_____

It is easy to envy what others have. The problem with this is it assumes that what you have is inferior to what you don't have. This is especially true with marriage and singleness. In reality, both have accompanying benefits and problems. Paul saw this in the Corinthian church, where there was tremendous pressure for sexual immorality and a sense of urgency about spreading the gospel. Single people wanted to be married to avoid sin, and married people wanted to have more time to serve God. Both singleness and marriage are gifts, with advantages and disadvantages to each. Both can be used to glorify God. Instead of worrying about what you don't have, thank God for what you have and focus on serving God where you are.

REALIZE
the principle

6 What do married people today envy about singleness?

_____

_____

_____

_____

7 What do single people today envy about marriage?

_____

_____

_____

_____

8 What are some of the reasons that marriage is to be entered into with care and much prayer?

_____

_____

_____

_____

9 What in our society makes it difficult to remain single?

_____

_____

_____

_____

10 What in our society makes it difficult to remain married?

_____

_____

_____

_____

11 Identify one specific area of marriage or singleness that you envy.

_____

_____

_____

_____

12 What makes it difficult for you to be content with your situation?

_____

_____

_____

_____

13 Pray and thank God for your singleness or marriage.

_____

_____

14 What opportunities do you have to use your singleness or marriage to glorify God?

RESOLVE
to take action

_____

_____

_____

_____

_____

_____

A What instructions did Paul give to married couples about their sexual relationship (7:1-5)? Why is it important to take these instructions seriously today?

MORE
for studying
other themes
in this section

B What reasons for divorce does Paul mention? When is divorce inappropriate? What plan of action would you suggest for a Christian who's in an unhappy marriage?

C In what ways are children of a believing parent "holy" (7:14)? What kind of parenting responsibilities does this imply?

D How do you think the Corinthians understood the phrase "the time is short" (7:29)? Time is even shorter now. In what ways might this fact affect your life-style?

E What are issues other than marriage in which it is sometimes difficult to be content?

F Based on this chapter, what advice would you give to a young person about to get married?

REFLECT
on your life

1 What personal rights and freedoms have been issues in the news recently?

_____
_____
_____

2 Describe a time when you had to stand up for your rights. How did you feel in that situation?

_____
_____
_____
_____
_____

READ
the passage

Read 1 Corinthians 8:1—9:18, the chart "Stronger, Weaker Believers" (chapter 9), and the following notes:

☐8:1 ☐8:4-9 ☐8:10-13 ☐9:4ff

3 What was the controversy in Corinth about meat that had been sacrificed to idols? (8:1-13)

_____
_____
_____
_____

4 What limitations did this place on the Corinthians' rights (8:9-13)?

_____

_____

_____

_____

5 What rights could Paul have insisted on (9:4-15)?

_____

_____

_____

_____

_____

6 What was more important to Paul than exercising his rights? (9:15-18)

_____

_____

_____

_____

In our society, people are expected to stand up for their rights and watch out for themselves. God's way is just the opposite. Though we have rights, there are certain values and priorities that take precedence over our rights. These include not hurting a brother or sister in Christ, not putting stumbling blocks in front of anyone, and, above all, doing what God has called us to do. We are to live with humility and love. As a mature Christian and a leader, Paul had freedom and rights.

REALIZE
the principle

7 Though eating food sacrificed to idols wasn't wrong, why did Paul counsel against it?

_____

_____

_____

_____

8 What are some modern-day equivalents to food sacrificed to idols?

_____

_____

_____

_____

_____

_____

RESPOND
to the message

9 Give some examples of how insisting on your rights can be a stumbling block to others.

_____

_____

_____

_____

_____

_____

10 When would it become necessary to limit your rights?

_____

_____

_____

_____

_____

11 What sensitivities of others would you want to be careful about offending?

_____

_____

_____

_____

_____

_____

12 Whom do you know who might be affected by your freedoms and rights?

_____

_____

_____

_____

13 What can you do to help that person grow in his/her faith?

_____

_____

_____

_____

_____

A What advantages and disadvantages can you see to someone providing for his/her own financial support while doing ministry? What can you do to support those in ministry?

B Why was it important for Paul to preach whether he wanted to or not (9:17, 18)? What areas of Christian responsibility are your duty to perform in much the same way?

C In this passage, who are stronger brothers and who are weaker brothers (8:7-13)? What responsibilities does each have toward the others? What responsibilities does this give you?

MORE
for studying
other themes
in this section

REFLECT
on your life

1 Choose one the following activities and tell what it would take to be excellent in it: ❏chess, ❏speed skating, ❏scientific research, ❏football, ❏piano, ❏writing, ❏carpentry.

_____

_____

_____

_____

_____

_____

READ
the passage

Read 1 Corinthians 9:19—11:1 and the following notes:

❏9:24-27 ❏9:27 ❏10:1-5 ❏10:7-10 ❏10:11 ❏10:16-21 ❏10:21 ❏10:23, 24
❏10:28-33 ❏10:31

2 What made Paul excellent at telling people about Christ (9:19-27)?

_____

_____

_____

_____

3 How did Paul choose his activities? (See 9:23, 27; 10:23-24, 31.)

_____

_____

_____

_____

_____

4 How did the people of Israel get sidetracked from their goal (10:1-13)?

_____

_____

_____

_____

_____

5 How would you describe Paul's purpose in life?

_____

REALIZE
the principle

_____

_____

_____

_____

Paul was a driven man. He had a clear sense of what was important and moved ahead accordingly. Paul knew that God had called him to share the good news about Christ, so he ordered his life around that purpose. Paul was motivated by the needs of people, his responsibility to use his gifts, and the knowledge that God would evaluate his life. As a result, he was dedicated to telling others about Christ. God has a unique calling and purpose for each of us. To be effective, we need to have a sense of purpose and to know where to focus our energies.

6 How does a person determine God's purpose for his/her life?

_____

_____

_____

_____

7 How does this purpose relate to the non-spiritual areas of life, such as home, school, work, and recreation?

_____

_____

_____

_____

_____

8 How can a person do "all for the glory of God" (10:31)?

_____

_____

_____

_____

_____

_____

RESPOND
to the message

9 If you could accomplish one thing for God during this life, what would it be?

_____

_____

_____

_____

_____

10 What resources (spiritual gifts, relationships, material possessions, time, education) has God given you to accomplish this goal?

_____

_____

_____

_____

_____

11 How can you bring more of your activities into line with God's purpose for your life?

_____

_____

_____

_____

_____

12 What changes do you need to make to become more focused toward God's purpose for your life?

_____

_____

_____

_____

_____

RESOLVE
to take action

13 What step can you take this week?

_____

_____

_____

_____

A What do the words *prize* and *crown* in 1 Corinthians 9:24-27 refer to? How can you make these more effective motivators in your life?

B What was Paul's method for sharing the gospel (9:19-23)? What's the difference between being "all things to all men" (9:22) and unhealthy compromise? In what ways can you make these adjustments for the sake of the gospel?

C What did Paul mean when he talked about the possibility of being disqualified (9:27)? What might this idea mean for you?

D The Israelites lost sight of their purpose even though God did miracles in their presence (10:3, 4). What does it take to keep your eyes on your purpose?

E How can a Christian drink both the cup of the Lord and the cup of demons (10:18-22)? How would this be possible in your life?

MORE
for studying
other themes
in this section

REFLECT
on your life

1 If you went to church as a child, jot down several adjectives that describe what you remember worship services being like.

_____

_____

_____

_____

2 Describe the ideal worship service today. What should be a part of every good worship service?

_____

_____

_____

_____

_____

READ
the passage

Read 1 Corinthians 11:2-34 and the following notes:

❑11:2-16 ❑11:3 ❑11:9-11 ❑11:14, 15 ❑11:21, 22 ❑11:27ff ❑11:27-34

3 How was the issue concerning head coverings affecting the Corinthians' worship (11:2-16)?

_____

_____

_____

_____

4 Describe the problems Paul addressed regarding the Lord's Supper. Why was this such a concern to him (11:17-34)?

_____

_____

_____

5 What do the issues of male/female relationships in worship and proper attitude toward the Lord's Supper have in common?

_____

_____

_____

_____

REALIZE
the principle

The Corinthians brought their problems to worship with them. Some of these problems, such as the matter of head coverings, involved disagreement over how they were being perceived by outsiders. Other problems, such as their abuse of the Lord's Supper, stemmed from broken relationships, pride, and self-centeredness. Paul wanted them to know that the attitudes they brought to worship and the way they acted during worship had great importance. In worship we come into God's presence and declare that we are his people, united together in faith. We can't do that if we are divided, fighting, or jockeying for the best seats. We must come into God's presence focused on him and unified as a group. We must worship with respect toward one another and toward God. Otherwise, we miss the purpose of coming together in the first place.

6 What conflicts and problems prevent churches from worshiping well?

_____

_____

_____

7 How would you evaluate a worship service?

_____

_____

_____

_____

RESPOND
to the message

8 What preoccupations sometimes hinder you from coming to worship services properly prepared?

_____

_____

_____

_____

_____

9 What could you do to eliminate those hindrances?

_____

_____

_____

_____

10 How might you improve the quality of your church's worship services?

_____

_____

_____

_____

11 How can you prepare for receiving the Lord's Supper?

_____

_____

_____

_____

12 What are one or two things you can do on Saturday nights or Sunday mornings to prepare for worship?

_____

_____

_____

_____

_____

_____

RESOLVE
to take action

13 What is one thing you can do to enhance the worship of your family or of those around you?

_____

_____

_____

_____

_____

A What does your church believe about the role of women in the church today? What changes would enable all people to participate in the life of the church?

B The Corinthians had to be careful about head coverings because of what such coverings meant to some people in their culture. What cultural practices should Christians be careful about because of what they mean to others?

C Some people were "weak and sick," and some had "fallen asleep" because of improper use of the Lord's Supper (11:30). What does it mean to partake of the Lord's Supper in a worthy manner?

MORE
for studying
other themes
in this section

REFLECT
on your life

1 What parts of your body are involved in changing a light bulb?

_____

_____

_____

_____

_____

2 Recall a time when you stubbed your toe. How did the injury affect your entire body?

_____

_____

_____

_____

_____

READ
the passage

Read 1 Corinthians 12:1-31 and the following notes:

❏ 12:12 ❏ 12:13 ❏ 12:14-24 ❏ 12:25, 26

3 In what ways is the church like a human body? (12:12-26)

_____

_____

_____

_____

_____

4 When does this body function at its best? (12:12-26)

_____

_____

_____

_____

_____

The Christians at Corinth saw certain spiritual gifts as more important than others. They thought that some Christians had highly important gifts, while others did not. God wanted them to know that he gives *every* Christian a vital function. None of us is small and unnecessary in God's kingdom. Each person has something vital to contribute. There are no unimportant or unnecessary people in the body of Christ because God has given each of us valuable gifts and abilities "for the common good" (12:7).

REALIZE
the principle

5 What causes us to value some gifts in the church more than others?

_____

_____

_____

_____

6 How can you tell when a church values all gifts equally?

_____

_____

_____

_____

RESPOND
to the message

7 What reasons do people have for not using their gifts for God's service?

_____

_____

_____

_____

_____

8 What gifts or roles in your church tend to be overlooked, unappreciated, or unrecognized?

_____

_____

_____

_____

9 What can be done to show appreciation for people whose gifts are usually overlooked?

_____

_____

_____

_____

10 How does a person discover what his/her role might be?

_____

_____

_____

_____

11 What gifts do you have that God wants you to use in the body of Christ?

_____

_____

_____

_____

_____

12 Whom can you commend this week for using their gifts in God's service? (Try to think of people whose gifts aren't ordinarily recognized.)

_____

_____

_____

_____

_____

_____

RESOLVE
to take action

13 What is one way you can use your unique gift(s) to serve the body of Christ this week?

_____

_____

_____

_____

_____

A Christians must be careful not to follow false teachers (12:1-3). What are ways to avoid being deceived by false teachers?

B What is a local church? What difference can a local church make in its community?

C What is the purpose of spiritual gifts (12:7)? How have you been able to use your gifts for this purpose?

D What are the "greater gifts" (12:31)? In what ways can your gifts fall under this category?

MORE
for studying
other themes
in this section

1 Who was your first childhood "love"?

REFLECT
on your life

_____

_____

_____

2 How has your understanding of love changed since then?

_____

_____

_____

_____

_____

Read 1 Corinthians 13:1-13 and the following notes:

❐ 13:1ff ❐13:4-7 ❐13:12 ❐13:13

READ
the passage

3 What good things can substitute for love (13:1-3)?

_____

_____

_____

_____

4 Why is love so important (13:1-3)?

_____

_____

_____

5 What symptoms show that love is missing (13:4-8)?

_____

_____

_____

6 What feature of love sets it apart from all the spiritual gifts (13:8-12)?

_____

_____

_____

_____

The Corinthian believers were very gifted people (1:7). In fact, they had impressive gifts such as prophecy, tongues, and faith. But the Corinthians were being unloving about the way they treated each other while taking pride in their gifts. They lived as if spiritual gifts were more important than love. But Paul points out that love is most important of all. No matter what your talents and abilities, what really matters to God is whether you demonstrate love toward others.

REALIZE
the principle

7 How would you summarize the description of love in this chapter?

_____

_____

_____

8 How has God demonstrated this kind of love?

_____

_____

_____

_____

9 What makes it difficult for us to love this way?

_____

_____

_____

_____

_____

10 How can Christians find the motivation and strength to love as they should?

_____

_____

_____

11 Many people talk about love, but there seem to be few loving people. What often takes the place of love in our society?

_____

_____

_____

_____

RESPOND
to the message

12 In the spirit of 1 Corinthians 13:1-3, fill in the blank with a talent or ability you have: "If I have the gift of _____, but have not love, I am nothing."

13 How could this gift be used in an unloving way?

_____

_____

_____

14 How could you exercise this gift in a loving way?

_____

_____

_____

15 When is it difficult for you to act in love toward someone close to you?

_____

_____

_____

16 What will it take for you to be more consistently loving toward others?

_____

_____

_____

_____

17 Think of one relationship in which you need to demonstrate love. What needs to change in your actions toward this person?

_____

_____

_____

_____

RESOLVE
to take action

18 What will you do for this person in the coming week?

_____

_____

_____

_____

A When will we no longer need spiritual gifts (13:9, 10)? How should we use them in the meantime? Who could benefit from this use of your gifts?

B What is hopeful about the future for Christians (13:8-12)? What about this encourages you? In what ways can your life reflect this hope now?

MORE
for studying
other themes
in this section

REFLECT
on your life

1 What spiritual gifts are used in a typical Sunday morning worship service at your church?

_____

_____

_____

_____

_____

2 What gifts did you use last Sunday at church during worship?

_____

_____

_____

_____

_____

READ
the passage

Read 1 Corinthians 14:1-40 and the following notes:

❒14:1 ❒14:2 ❒14:22-25 ❒14:26ff ❒14:33

3 What kinds of gifts should believers desire (14:1, 12, 39)?

_____

_____

_____

_____

4 How should all gifts be used? (See 14:2-12, 26-32, 38, 39.)

_____

_____

_____

_____

5 In what ways should we limit our use of spiritual gifts? (See 14:13-19, 27-32.)

_____

_____

_____

_____

_____

6 What is the relationship between the way we worship and the purpose of worship?

_____

REALIZE
the principle

_____

_____

_____

All of our spiritual gifts, talents, and abilities are given by God for the benefit of others. Our spiritual gifts are specifically for building up our brothers and sisters in Christ. God expects us to use them for this purpose. Because the believers in Corinth were spiritually immature, they were using their gifts to help themselves rather than others. As a result, when they gathered together for worship, they were divided rather than unified. God wants us to use our spiritual gifts to help and build up his people. Instead of expecting people to give to you, or focusing your gifts on yourself, use God's gifts to benefit others.

7 How does a believer's spiritual maturity affect the way he/she uses spiritual gifts in worship?

_____

_____

_____

_____

_____

8 This chapter is linked to the previous chapter with the statement, "Follow the way of love and eagerly desire spiritual gifts" (14:1). In what ways are love and spiritual gifts related?

_____

_____

_____

_____

_____

_____

RESPOND
to the message

9 What opportunities do people in your church have to discover and put their gifts into practice?

_____

_____

_____

_____

_____

10 What are some ways you can make sure that worship in your church is "done in a fitting and orderly way" (14:40)?

_____

_____

_____

_____

11 How can you use your spiritual gifts to enhance worship and help others?

_____

_____

_____

_____

_____

12 What spiritual gifts of yours can be used in worship?

_____

_____

_____

_____

RESOLVE
to take action

13 What spiritual leader in your church could help you find a way to use your gifts in the church?

_____

_____

_____

_____

_____

A What does it mean for women to be silent in the church? What is the role of women in your church? How does your church interpret these passages and make a place for women to fully use their spiritual gifts?

B What is the function of prophecy in the New Testament? How does it compare to Old Testament prophecy? If you have the gift of prophecy, how can you exercise it responsibly in your church?

C Paul referred to his writing as "the Lord's command" (14:37). In what unique ways do you treat the Scriptures, God's inspired words to us?

MORE
for studying
other themes
in this section

REFLECT
on your life

1 What is heaven like?

_____

_____

_____

_____

2 What are you looking forward to about heaven? What are you apprehensive about?

_____

_____

_____

_____

READ
the passage

Read 1 Corinthians 15:1-58, the chart "Physical and Resurrection Bodies" (chapter 16), and the following notes:

❏15:5-8 ❏15:12ff ❏15:13-18 ❏15:19 ❏15:30-34 ❏15:35ff ❏15:42-44

❏15:45 ❏15:58

3 Why is it so important to the Christian faith that Jesus Christ rose physically from the grave? (15:12-19)

_____

_____

_____

4 What would be the implications for our faith if the resurrection were a hoax? (15:17-19)

_____

_____

_____

_____

5 When will death finally be defeated (15:20-28)?

_____

_____

_____

6 What will our resurrected bodies be like (15:35-49)?

_____

_____

_____

7 How should belief in the resurrection of Christ influence how a Christian lives?

_____

REALIZE
the principle

_____

_____

Nothing is more important to the Christian faith than the truth of the resurrection of Jesus. Because Jesus was actually raised physically, all his people will be raised to eternal glory as well. This isn't just a theoretical doctrine for Christians to discuss. Christ's resurrection puts everything in a new perspective. Life and death, work and recreation, values and priorities, all look different when viewed in light of the resurrection that is to come. Because Christ lives, you can live now with confidence in God and hope in the future.

8 What is the evidence for the resurrection of Jesus?

_____

_____

_____

9 Why does the truth of Christ's resurrection give Christians hope?

_____

_____

_____

_____

_____

10 What do you think would cause people to deny the resurrection of Christ?

_____

_____

_____

_____

_____

_____

RESPOND
to the message

11 In what situations would you use the story of Jesus' resurrection to give some-one hope?

_____

_____

_____

_____

_____

_____

12 How would you answer someone who says that the resurrection of Christ is just a matter of faith?

_____

_____

_____

_____

_____

13 What changes would occur in your life if you began to live more fully in light of the resurrection to come?

_____

_____

_____

_____

_____

_____

14 As a Christian, you have a reason for hope. How does this hope affect the way you live?

_____

_____

_____

_____

_____

RESOLVE
to take action

15 In what situations can belief in the resurrection give you comfort and hope?

_____

_____

_____

_____

_____

A What is the baptism for the dead (15:29)? What happens to people after they die? How can this message help a believer in Christ? How can it help an unbeliever?

B Compare our present bodies with our resurrection bodies (15:35-49). How are they similar? How are they different? What are some of the limitations of our physical bodies? How can we use our bodies to glorify God?

C What does it mean for us that Jesus is the "last Adam" (15:22, 45-49)?

D What will happen when Christ returns (15:50-54)? What can you do now to prepare for that event?

MORE
for studying
other themes
in this section

REFLECT
on your life

1 Who has made a significant difference in your life?

_____

_____

_____

_____

_____

_____

2 What did this person do that made such a difference?

_____

_____

_____

_____

_____

_____

READ
the passage

Read 1 Corinthians 16:1-24 and the following notes:

☐16:1-4 ☐16:13, 14 ☐16:19 ☐16:22 ☐16:24

3 According to this chapter, in what ways were people involved in Paul's ministry or in ministry in general?

_____

_____

_____

_____

4 What do Paul's personal requests reveal about him? (16:5-11)

_____

_____

_____

_____

Paul seldom ministered alone. In all of his travels and missionary ventures, he was in the company of trusted and valued friends. Some of his lowest times came when he was isolated. In spite of Paul's great gifts and calling, he recognized his need for fellowship and support. He depended on others for help and encouragement. These supportive people were his partners in ministry. God calls all of us as Christians to be involved in ministry; we are partners together with Christ and other believers. How incredible to realize that God calls us to partnership in the building of his kingdom!

REALIZE
the principle

5 What are the benefits of being involved with other people in ministry?

_____

_____

_____

_____

_____

6 What consequences might there be for people who minister by themselves?

_____

_____

_____

_____

7 What are some of the unique needs of ministry leaders?

_____

_____

_____

_____

_____

RESPOND
to the message

8 In what ministries do you have a support role?

_____

_____

_____

_____

9 In what ministries do you have a leadership role?

_____

_____

_____

_____

10 Who are some people who have been a part of a "life-support system" for you in your Christian life?

_____

_____

_____

_____

11 What are some ways that your church can encourage and support the people involved in leadership in your church?

_____

_____

_____

_____

12 What leaders in your church can you encourage or support—a pastor, a small group leader, elders, deacons, church school teachers, or others?

_____

_____

_____

_____

_____

_____

RESOLVE
to take action

13 Choose at least one person from the above list and write down how you will encourage him/her this week.

_____

_____

_____

_____

_____

A What do Paul's instructions to the Corinthians in 1 Corinthians 16:1-3 suggest about how Christians should give? What can you do to support God's work with your money?

B What do you learn about Paul's ministry from 1 Corinthians 16:5-9? Paul says "a great door for effective work" has opened to him in Ephesus (1 Corinthians 16:9). What factors may have led him to conclude this? How might opposition affect your ministry for Christ?

C How did Paul end this difficult letter to the church at Corinth (16:19-24)? What can this teach us about confronting problems with others?

D Paul longed for the Lord's return (16:22)? How did this affect Paul's ministry? What effect does the promise of Christ's return have on your life?

MORE
for studying
other themes
in this section